*preaching
and parish renewal*

WALLACE E. FISHER

preaching
and parish renewal

NASHVILLE • NEW YORK   ℬ ABINGDON PRESS

PREACHING AND PARISH RENEWAL

Copyright © 1966 by Abingdon Press

Library of Congress Catalog Card Number: 66-22916

SET UP, PRINTED, AND BOUND BY THE
PARTHENON PRESS, AT NASHVILLE,
TENNESSEE, UNITED STATES OF AMERICA

FOR MY WIFE
Margaret

AND OUR SON
Mark

preface

Parish renewal in the Lutheran Church of the Holy Trinity, Lancaster, Pennsylvania, and the sustenance of its new life are inextricably bound up with biblical preaching. The staff, official board, parishioners, and many in the community share this conviction. We are convinced that parish renewal and biblical preaching are inseparable. That is the immediate reason for this book. Another reason is the pressing need to say a good word for preaching itself. Our experience at Trinity Church affirms Paul's witness: "It was God's good pleasure through the foolishness of the preaching to save them that believe" (I Cor. 1:21 ASV).

What we mean by "biblical preaching" is defined in Part I, The Case for Preaching. It is illustrated by the sermons in Part II, The Gospel and Human Nature, and in Part III, The Gospel and the World. Part IV, Beyond the Pulpit, demonstrates briefly how one preacher addresses the gospel to pluralistic gatherings (service clubs, P.T.A.'s, public school and college commencements, military gatherings, etc.). A brief statement on each sermon identifies the year it was preached, describes the prevailing mind in Trinity Church when it was preached, sets down its objectives, and hints at the dialogue which ensued. Similar statements introduce the addresses. Three appendices also reflect the dialogue in and beyond the parish.

It is evident at this critical juncture in the life of the American church that there can be "popular" preaching without the Word of the Lord confronting anyone. There can be prosperous institutions apart from prophetic preaching. There can be "correct theology" without a trace of new life surging through the church. There can be "social action" without Christ. And there can be so much talk about, and experimentation with, "new forms" that this too becomes another "activity" by which churchmen escape existential involvements in God's world. *New life* in any parish comes by the Holy Spirit through the living Word confronting persons through persons. This essential confrontation employs many different human activities. Preaching is one of the most significant.

Parishioners and colleagues at Trinity have called persistently for printed sermons. Several hundred different mimeographed and taped sermons have been made available to them. But, except for eight sermons commandeered for publication across the years, I have not been disposed heretofore to provide sermons for publication. Living with the hard discipline of preaching two and three times weekly in the same parish for a decade and a half and steadily "on the circuit," I know firsthand that a sermon is an act of worship and witness, a form dependent on the context of the service, the person of the preacher, and the verbal means of communication. The sermons included here—expository, doctrinal, topical, textual—reflect something of a particular congregation's rising response to, and participation in, biblical preaching as acts of worship and witness. They are one aspect of the recurring Event of Christ.

Consequently, *Preaching and Parish Renewal* seeks to retain something of the oral presentations at Trinity, in college and university chapels, for missions to military personnel, and at denominational and interdenominational gatherings. It profits from the subsequent spoken and written response to these sermons. The introductory section on preaching has also been tested "where the action is": in clergy conferences from coast to coast and as a lecture for my graduate students at the Lancaster (United Church of Christ) Theological Seminary. This book, therefore, is not simply a collection of "favorite" sermons. It is a case study on preaching in and beyond the parish, 1953-1965.

More specifically, the sermons were selected to illustrate one strand in parish renewal. The book will offer sharper insights if it is read in the perspective provided by my account of the renewal of a center city church, the Lutheran Church of the Holy Trinity, the oldest church (1730) in the oldest inland city in the United States, Lancaster, Pennsylvania. Abingdon Press suggested this book as a sequel to that account, *From Tradition to Mission* (Abingdon, 1965).

The secretaries at Trinity Church, Mrs. Arline S. Fellenbaum, and especially my secretary, Mrs. Charles D. Flowers, deserve thanks for preparing the manuscript. Jack R. Hoffman and Larry L. Lehman, ordained associates at Trinity; Hugo W. Schroeder, Jr., and Harald S. Sigmar, valued friends in the ministry; and these parishioners—Wilfred P. Bennett, John B. Byers, Ruth Grigg Horting, Ann Haagen Musselman, J. Albert Seldomridge, Ann Bolbach White, and Robert H. Witmer, M.D. —have read the manuscript, offering valuable comments. Their enthusiastic participation in Trinity's preaching-teaching ministry is, of course, their most significant contribution.

WALLACE E. FISHER

contents

IV. *Beyond the Pulpit*

I

the case for preaching

For, "*every one who calls upon the name of the Lord will be saved.*"
But how are men to call upon him in whom they have not be-
lieved? And how are they to believe in him of whom they have
never heard? And how are they to hear without a preacher?

—*Paul (Rom. 10:13-14)*

It was God's good pleasure through the foolishness of the preaching to
save them that believe.

—*Paul (I Cor. 1:21 ASV)*

The Case for Preaching

Two residents of New England, separated by less than a century, confront the contemporary preacher with conflicting judgments on the significance of the pulpit. Phillips Brooks, at the close of the nineteenth century, viewed preaching as the best medium for communicating God's truth to persons through a person. Pointing to the rigors of the pulpit and recognizing that no man apart from Christ is equal to them, Brooks declared his confidence in God's power to change man through the human activity of preaching the gospel.[1]

Three quarters of a century later, Peter Berger, professor of sociology at Hartford Seminary in Connecticut, argued that the pulpit is no longer significant, that any clergyman who thinks preaching influences laymen on the other six days of the week is deluded![2] Professor Berger's critique is accepted and supported, not only in the world, but in many quarters of the church.

There are clergy who regard preaching as being less significant than other functions of ministry. They admit readily to a low view of their work in the pulpit. Apparently it is easier for them to deplore the inhospitable cultural climate for preaching, to view the laity as unresponsive "listeners," and to flee the study in response to other pastoral duties, than it is for them to admit that no cultural situation has ever been hospitable to gospel preaching, that unconverted parishioners are not moved by polite homilies, and that biblical preaching is a primary pastoral duty. Paul Althaus struck a sensitive nerve when he

[1] *On Preaching* (Paperback ed.; New York: The Seabury Press, 1964).
[2] *The Noise of Solemn Assemblies* (Garden City: Doubleday & Company, 1961), p. 37.

15

observed that people today are not tired of preaching; they are tired of *our* preaching.[3] The enthusiastic response of laymen to Leslie Weatherhead, Peter Marshall, W. E. Sangster, D. T. Niles, and Helmut Thielicke in the postwar era supports his critique. But effective preaching is hard work! Some clergy refuse to give it the costly toil that it requires.

The late Ernest Fremont Tittle, writing more than three decades ago, identified lack of work as one cause of ineffectual preaching.

Too many preachers are lying down on the job. . . . The time which they do spend among their books, or to speak more accurately, in the same room with their books—what do they do with it? Mostly they kill it. . . . Except in communities that are obviously and wickedly over-churched, and except also in those far too numerous instances where churches are poorly located, if the church is empty it is largely because the preacher is empty.[4]

A quarter of a century later, Roy Pearson, dean of the Andover-Newton Theological School was equally pointed: "If God needs the preacher's heart, He also needs his head. . . . When the minister stops studying, he simply stops. The world moves quickly beyond him." [5] Books do not make the preacher any more than clothes make the man. But the diligent, dogged, daily study of God's Word, disciplined listening to and dialogue with the world, and sustained periods of hard theological thinking are prerequisites for relevant preaching. Faith is no substitute for hard work.

It is ironic in this age of mass communication that the church —whose Lord preached to eager multitudes and whose seasons

[3] John W. Doberstein in Helmut Thielicke, *The Waiting Father* (New York: Harper & Row, 1959), p. 7.

[4] *The Foolishness of Preaching* (New York: Henry Holt & Company, 1930), pp. 304-5.

[5] *The Ministry of Preaching* (New York: Harper & Brothers, 1959), pp. 77-78.

of splendid involvement with the world are identifiable with its seasons of vigorous preaching—declines to work at preaching to assemblies of persons. The lay academy, the coffeehouse, the Bible study group, the school of lay theology, the pastoral counseling center, and the church school *are* arenas where persons can meet Christ face to face; they *are* means whereby Christ can confront the world.[6] Alert parish pastors do employ these "new" forms to communicate the gospel to small groups.[7] But they do not neglect preaching to large assemblies. They are convinced, as Kierkegaard was, that the Word "divides a crowd into individuals." The Word in preaching *does* reach out, lay hold on, and motivate persons, even as those persons are in the midst of a crowd.

The current disposition to denigrate preaching—the formal act of heralding the good news to one hundred or one thousand people in a sanctuary—weakens the church's God-given ministry. Forthright biblical preaching which avoids the marginal (shallow moralism) and penetrates to the heart of man's profound dilemma (guilt and meaninglessness) and speaks to his loneliness persuades persons to repent, encourages them to trust God, and gives them identity. Linked with evangelical teaching, it motivates and equips them to exercise Christ's ministry in the world. Apart from biblical preaching, worship becomes esoteric or perfunctory; the sacraments are viewed as cultic rites or mechanical tests for membership; evangelism remains a human activity; stewardship is equated with "raising the budget." The neglect of biblical preaching weakens the church's witness because it violates the biblical image of ministry.

[6] These ventures are not new. John Wesley was converted in a Bible study group two centuries ago. Luther's *Table Talk* suggests a "house school" of theology. The pastoral counselor was much in demand during the "age of pietism."

[7] Wallace E. Fisher, *From Tradition to Mission* (Nashville: Abingdon Press, 1965), See especially chapter 4, "Dialogue and Encounter," and chapter 5, "Dynamics for Outreach," for a firsthand account of the use of different media for communicating the gospel in small groups at times other than the "Sunday school hour."

Preaching in the New Testament

Jesus came preaching. That is the clear picture Luke got from Jesus' contemporaries. (Luke 4:42-44.) Mark learned in the pristine Christian community how Jesus valued and employed the activity of preaching: "Now after John was arrested, Jesus came into Galilee, preaching the gospel of God, and saying, 'The time is fulfilled, and the kingdom of God is at hand; repent, and believe in the gospel'" (Mark 1:14-15). At the outset of Jesus' ministry, he declared that the prophecy of Isaiah was fulfilled: "God sent me to *proclaim* release to the captives" (Luke 4:6-19).

Jesus was a magnificent preacher. Wherever he preached, the Gospel accounts testify, crowds thronged to hear him. People talked about him incessantly. They concluded from his preaching that he knew God, man, and the world intimately—and loved all three. Consequently, many listened eagerly to his teaching, clamored for his ministry of cure, and sought his pastoral counseling. Others, especially the professional religionists, green with envy, excited their Roman overlords, who were committed to keeping the peace at any price, by suggesting the likelihood of insurrection at the hands of this persuasive preacher.[8]

There is an incalculable difference between Jesus' preaching and contemporary preaching. Many well-educated preachers who rely on neatly constructed, artfully illustrated homilies delivered cautiously to bland, white congregations have little in common with that robust and radical preacher from Galilee. Ignoring or rejecting the image of ministry which Jesus embodied and projected, many contemporary preachers take in-

---

[8] I acknowledge my debt to Rudolph Bultmann, but I am not an uncritical follower. Bultmann's attractive plea obscures the crucial truth that the gospel differs from *all* mythology in that its essence, Christ, is datable; that his ministry is an enacted event; that in him my salvation is accomplished.

stead as their model the corporation executive, the educationist, the social reformer, the liturgical revivalist, the psychological counselor.[9] Consequently, their preaching does not "leave completely undistorted and uncompromised the great, wonderful and mysterious fact that God has spoken to us in his Son, Jesus Christ our Lord." [10]

The radical difference between twentieth-century preaching and first-century preaching comes into sharp focus when the diplomatic ways of many contemporary preachers are compared with the bold thrusts of those first-century preachers—Peter, Paul, and Stephen. The former are elected to service clubs; the latter were arrested for disturbing the peace, run out of town, or murdered. Contrast the casual congregational response to much contemporary preaching with the concerned, angry, violent response to the preaching of those men. Peter's congregation, cut to the heart, cried out, "What shall we do to be saved?" Paul's messages so infuriated the silversmiths in Ephesus that he had to leave town. Stephen's forthright preaching led to his murder.

The conclusion is inescapable: Christ confronts persons through preachers who, making themselves willing habitations for him, proclaim God's demands and promises no matter what the cost may be to their persons. That is how the church was planted in a pagan world, renewed in the sixteenth century, empowered to ameliorate social conditions in eighteenth-century England, and enabled to resist, sporadically, the might of the Nazi state. Those critics who argue that preaching is one function of ministry which, like Custer on the plains of Dakota, made its last stand at the close of the nineteenth century, are guilty of superficial judgment. Paul Althaus is closer to the

[9] H. Richard Niebuhr, *The Purpose of the Church and Its Ministry* (New York: Harper & Row, 1956), pp. 82 ff.

[10] John March in Karl Barth, *Deliverance to the Captives* (New York: Harper & Row, 1961), p. 9.

truth: people are not weary of preaching; they are tired of *our* preaching. It still pleases God to save persons through the "foolishness of preaching" when it is done by men who bring his Word to bear on postmodern man's elemental needs.

The Foolishness of Preaching

Responsible preachers are cultural realists. They ask who listens to preaching these days and how it is useful to those who do. They wrestle with questions such as C. E. M. Joad thrust at the Church of England three decades ago, "Will the world ever listen to you again?" [11] Authentic preachers are not neatly grooved individuals who "go along to get along." They, perhaps more than others, inquire agonizingly how any mortal can presume to preach in this "time between the times." They ask how the gospel of God, communicated through the human activity of preaching, can compete with the rival gospels of status, sex, organization-mindedness, and nationalism—especially when the impact of these rivals is magnified a million times by radio, television, and paperback publishing. Responsible parish pastors wrestle with the complex aspects of relevant ministry in the world.[12]

But these questions are not new. They were being asked long before the present generation of critics made a profitable business of asking them and some clergy showed signs of being pathologically preoccupied with them. Four decades ago George A. Buttrick, delivering the Lyman Beecher lectures at Yale, observed that

our era is strewn with lay pulpits. In every sober magazine, in many a newspaper and novel, on the lecture-platform and the stage, the preacher (self-installed if not self-ordained) mounts the steps, hurls

[11] R. A. Edwards, *The Church and the World* (London: SCM Press, 1943), p. 1.
[12] It is concerned clergy and laymen who purchase the critical works of Winter, Berger, Robinson, Marty, Cox, *et al.*

his anathemas with all the dogmatism alleged to be characteristic of the calling, and brings down his fist with a resounding thump. . . . With preachers everywhere, why maintain a special order? . . . To many he is a pathetic figure, an anachronism, . . . wearing the expression of a startled rabbit.[13]

Questions on the relevance of preaching are as old as the first generation of Christians. It is true, however, that the contemporary preacher's task has become comparatively more difficult than it was for his predecessors in the nineteenth century. Today the educated world suspects, and in many quarters is convinced, that the Christian message is obsolete. During the twentieth century Schleiermacher's cadre of "cultured despisers" has become a mighty army. Furthermore, the missionary thrust of the church, which has not kept pace with the "population explosion," has been overmatched by the zeal of other world religions. Consequently, most segments of world society have little knowledge of Christianity as a religion. Only a minority of the world's population claim a personal relationship with Christ. Hordes of spiritually displaced persons populate the onetime "Christian countries." The parish itself has become a primary mission field.[14] At the close of the nineteenth century a perceptive churchman, Marcus Dods, observed: "I do not envy those who will carry the banner of Christianity in the twentieth century. . . . Yes, perhaps I do, but it will be a stiff fight." The fight has been "stiffer" than Dr. Dods suspected!

Questions on the relevance of preaching and of the church itself root deep in the crisis of our culture. Reformation man initiated no serious dialogue with Renaissance man. Bacon, Descartes, and Newton—men of Christian piety—unwittingly widened the breach during the seventeenth century. By the

[13] *Jesus Came Preaching* (New York: Charles Scribner's Sons, 1931), pp. 3-4.
[14] See Fisher, *From Tradition to Mission,* chapters 1-4, for a clinical report on a particular city church.

eighteenth century Hume's skepticism and Jefferson's "religious rationalism" were firmly lodged in Western culture. Nineteenth-century Europe produced Freidrich Nietzsche, Karl Marx, and Sigmund Freud. Nietzsche, pronouncing God dead, called for a revision of all values. Marx, espousing dialectical materialism and openly attacking Christianity as the "opiate of the people," laid the foundation for a new sociopolitical order. Freud, denying man's transcendental qualities, caricatured him as being exclusively naturalistic.

The disciples of Nietzsche, Marx, and Freud gained the upper hand. Their vigorous critiques of man and society, coupled with their bold remedies, fell in the fertile soil of a rapidly deteriorating historical situation in the West. Two devastating world wars, an enervating economic depression that shook the social foundations of the industrial nations, the advent of nuclear weapons powerful enough to obliterate entire metropolises, Asia in ferment and Africa in revolt—all this disheartened and in some quarters overwhelmed the institutional church. Wave after wave of fierce persecutions, beginning with the Bolsheviks and embracing the terrible decade of the Nazis, ruthlessly tore whole limbs from the body of Christ or domesticated his followers. These towering defeats, linked with the secularization of life inside the church in the West, made it appear that God was dead. Millions of people—confused, rootless, desperate—found the gospel according to Nietzsche, Marx, or Freud more relevant than the gospel of God.[15]

[15] The phrase, "God is dead," is presently receiving attention in theological circles and popular journals. Actually, this is not so much a "school of thought" as it is a cliché that is associated with several different contemporary theological thrusts in which three names are prominent: Paul Van Buren, linguistic analyst, who proposes that the traditional religious semantics are dead; Thomas J. J. Altizer, who dramatically points to what he calls the fact of God's death in our time; and William Hamilton, who attempts to explicate for our day some of the obscure insights included in the prison witness of Bonhoeffer, namely, that in a religionless commitment to Christ we have the freedom anywhere and everywhere to be "the man for others."

When the parish pastor at mid-century argues that the nineteenth-century clergy preached in a less demanding cultural setting, he is recognizing reality. When he believes that the Word in preaching refashions persons whom God enables to transform their culture, he is standing in the New Testament tradition. That is the authentic preacher's proper stance.

The Authentic Preacher

Certainly no man is able to herald God's gospel persuasively unless he is under God's call to preach. The kingdom of God does not rely on self-appointed ambassadors. The King's man, under direct appointment, inquires daily of his Lord how he can be a better citizen of the kingdom and a more influential ambassador. He does not excuse his ignorance of far-reaching cultural problems by pleading the press of parish duties, an evasion which unconverted parishioners will accept as long as "their" minister soothes their battered egos and approves their little worlds of self-interest. Instead, God's ambassador is alert to the subtle pressures to accommodate the gospel to his culture. Equally, he is on guard against his own stubborn disposition to avoid disciplined biblical study, hard theological thinking, and rugged person-to-person encounters which God expects of him.

The herald of God is concerned. He works at understanding the cultural situation in which the Word *and* its bearer must make their way. He also nurtures his "new life" from the Word. He has discovered that unless the God he proclaims is allowed to authenticate himself in the person of the preacher, his witness will be blunted. He is haunted by Richard Baxter's warning, "Beware lest you be void of the saving grace that you offer to others." [16]

[16] *The Reformed Pastor*, a seventeenth-century classic, belongs in every preacher's library.

Contemporary culture's preoccupation with communication, as though it were primarily a matter of form rather than of content and personhood, reveals how severely post modern man is alienated from God, himself, and others.[17] Any preacher who is captive to this sick culture can go through the motions of preaching, sometimes quite impressively, but the Word of the Lord does not confront persons through *his* person. The effective preacher testifies not only from and to the common Faith but also from and to *his* firsthand experience of Christ. His preaching is report and event. He demonstrates that the God of Abraham and Moses, of Jeremiah and Jesus, of Paul and Wesley, is at work in him. In this sense

the best sermons come from men whose wholesome personality, vigorous manhood, alert mind, and Christian consecration are gathered up in a power to communicate based less on cleverness of strategy than on achievement in being. It is the total man who is the bearer of the gospel, and in any aspirant to pulpit power the preparation of the sermon is far less important than the preparation of the self.[18]

No preacher comes easily to this confidence in the saving power of God through the "foolishness of preaching." Like any other mortal, he must be converted and grow in his understanding of God, self, and others.[19] The preacher's daily encounters with contemporary man's frantic efforts to find freedom, meaning, and God are not formal exercises; he too has traveled these highways. But he is no longer lost; *Christ has found him.* That is *what* he preaches; that is *why* he preaches. Having discovered the gospel's relevance for *his* person, he becomes a willing servant of the Word. "The necessity of preach-

[17] See Sören Kierkegaard, *Fear and Trembling; and the Sickness unto Death* (Anchor Book; Garden City: Doubleday & Company, 1954).

[18] Pearson, *The Ministry of Preaching*, p. 83.

[19] C. H. Dodd, "The Mind of Paul: I," in *New Testament Studies* (New York: Charles Scribner's Sons), concludes that Paul grew steadily in self-understanding.

ing resides in the fact that when God saves a man through Christ he insists on a living, personal encounter with him here and now in the sphere of present personal relationships." [20]

Finally, God's spokesman struggles to accept the fact of his preaching. Unlike the pulpiteer who "has an itch which only an audience can scratch," God's ambassador goes out reluctantly.[21] He has discovered pain as well as joy in this function of Christ's ministry. He has learned that those who reject the Word often reject its bearer; and like every human, he wants to be loved. (Jer. 2:8.) Consequently, the servant of the Word will lament occasionally, "Woe is me because I am called to preach the gospel in its offense and healing." The authentic preacher does not covet the preaching ministry, is never altogether comfortable in it, exercises it because the love of Christ constrains him. "Preaching," says Karl Barth, "is an act of daring, and only the man who would rather not preach and cannot escape from it ought ever to attempt it." [22] Luther confessed from the pulpit occasionally that he would escape preaching if he could.[23] Who can forget Jeremiah's anguished argument against God's call to preach, "I am only a youth" (1:6). Yet he did not escape the hound of heaven. "Thou hast persuaded me and I was persuaded." (20:7 ASV.)

Biblical preaching is not reserved for an intellectual elite who choose to preach as a favor to God. He chooses, calls, persuades, and equips his ambassadors. The task, therefore, is within the reach of any committed person who, possessed of emotional resilience and intellectual curiosity, accepts God's authority, honors his demands, claims his promises, and *works* at preaching. The

[20] H. H. Farmer, *The Servant of the Word* (New York: Charles Scribner's Sons, 1942), p. 27.
[21] Pearson, *The Ministry of Preaching*, p. 62.
[22] Quoted by Harry F. Baughman, *Jeremiah Today* (Philadelphia: Muhlenberg Press, 1947), p. 37.
[23] Roland H. Bainton, *Here I Stand* (Nashville: Abingdon Press, 1950), p. 349.

style of preaching varies from one man to another, but wherever ministers are alert, responsive, and faithful to the Word, people know from their preaching that the kingdom of God is at hand. Some come forward asking, "What must I do to become a citizen of the kingdom?" Others are indifferent. Some are hostile, rejecting the gospel and its bearer. All three responses testify to biblical preaching.

The gospel preacher—convinced by the Holy Spirit that the saving power of God comes through preaching and constrained by Christ's love to take it up—accepts God's strategy for exercising this function of ministry. God's strategy is simple. The preacher proclaims the whole Word which judges before it heals. God's strategy is realistic. The preacher teaches men that repentance and evangelical faith are inseparable.[24] Persons must be motivated to accept Christ's Lordship before they can be motivated and equipped to exercise his ministry. Too many clergy get the cart before the horse; they recruit, organize, and direct unconverted church members. Only as men are truly confronted with the whole gospel of God will some repent, believe, learn, witness, serve.

Inevitably, therefore, those clergy who accept God's strategy for preaching encounter stubborn resistance in pious-secular American communities. This resistance roots in a brand of "pietism" which treats Jesus with respect but avoids personal involvement with him, venerates the Bible but does not study it critically to discern its witness to the Word, and honors the church as a christening, marrying, burying society—a "holy place" filled with memories more sentimental than sacred. Like Phariseeism in Jesus' day and the "works righteousness" of the late Middle Ages, this human "pietism" acknowledges God while subtly disavowing his will and presuming on his grace.

---

[24] Jesus called men to repent and believe. The apostolic church, accepting Christ as Lord and Savior, proclaimed, "Repent, believe. The kingdom of God is at hand."

Divine grace is cheapened, because the gospel is robbed of ethical instruction.

As every minister who accepts God's strategy knows, the forthright preaching of the demands and promises of God creates tension, stirs controversy, incites conflict, and in some situations brings about the rejection of the gospel and its bearer. That is as true in a religionized culture as it is in a pagan culture, for it is the genius of gospel preaching to expose human piety as a deadly enemy of true Christianity. When this exposure is accomplished, some are infuriated, others are entertained, some are indifferent, others are set to hard thinking. Dialogue with the pulpit is under way. Tension and conflict, irritation and hostility, perception and insight, rejection and acceptance, understanding and growth, surge unevenly through the parish.[25]

We are not suggesting that the form, construction, and delivery of the sermon are unimportant. The man who mouths his words, stares at the opposite wall of the sanctuary as he preaches, neglects to order his thoughts so that his listeners can follow the course of his sermon, or has no serious thoughts at all, is not a herald of the gospel. On the other hand, the well-constructed sermon, artfully illustrated and graciously delivered (with or without manuscript), is not necessarily a vehicle for God's Word to man. Bernard Shaw's scathing judgment of W. E. Henley—that he possessed marvelous powers of expression but lacked anything significant to say—is applicable to far too many preachers these days.

The authentic preacher is a servant of the Word, a disciplined soldier willing to accept God's orders, an intelligent, intelligible witness to Christ.

[25] See Fisher, *From Tradition to Mission,* especially chapter 3 on preaching, "Confrontation and Response," for a firsthand account of this response in a particular parish.

Guideposts for Preaching

Effective biblical preaching is an affair of the mind and will as well as of the heart. The preacher needs guideposts throughout his ministry.[26]

Honesty. Some able preachers have suggested that a man ought to preach only what he knows firsthand of Christ.[27] In one sense that is true. We have argued that one communicates the Word of God with power if he has accepted Christ as *his* Savior and follows him as *his* Lord. But total commitment is beyond any man. Paul saw only through "a glass darkly." To preach, especially in the first decade of one's ministry, no more than what one has experienced of Christ would warp the objective character of the gospel.

The intended thrust in the plea that one should preach what he knows of Christ is on this order. The preacher will give himself to the Word in disciplined fashion. He will tend to the wellsprings of his own faith, searching the Scriptures for God's Word to him. He will seek to do Christ's commandments. The authentic preacher is a witness to God's truth, a steward of the gospel, a servant of the Word.

Either the preacher is content with this subordinate status or he is not. If he is, he discovers that humbling himself, he is exalted. If he is not, the answer is not to be found in hypocrisy—preaching as truth a way of life in which he disbelieves. Nor is it to be found in compromise—confining his proclamation to the incidental periphery of the gospel with which he has not quarreled and thus preaching the part as if it were the whole. If the preacher cannot preach the gospel in the untrammeled assurance that it contains the very word of life, he

[26] My indebtedness to these servants of the Word is too extensive to trace: Baxter, Brooks, Buttrick, Farmer, Fosdick, Gossip, Jowett, Sangster, Stewart, and Scherer.

[27] Theodore P. Ferris, *Go Tell the People* (New York: Charles Scribner's Sons, 1951), p. 86.

ought not to preach at all, or he ought to preach from a platform and not a pulpit.[28]

Honesty also requires accurate statements and truthful illustrations in and outside the pulpit. The preacher who, seeking dramatic effect, claims another's experience as his own may prove to be untrustworthy in keeping the parochial records, administering a staff ministry, or counseling another man's wife. Certainly, he will not be effective in the pulpit.

Humanity. The ordained minister recognizes and acknowledges that he is in the same situation as those to whom he ministers. He shares their humanity, knows it, admits it. He too has dark nights of the soul. He is no stranger to pride, impatience, arrogance, anger, bitterness, hatred, envy, lust, greed. He needs and claims God's acceptance, forgiveness, support, and love, as does any other parishioner whom he serves. He declines to use his preaching as a screen between God and his person or between himself and other selves. He is a sinner who, justified by faith, lives by grace. The clergyman is not a holy man; he is a human servant of the holy God. He seeks to be an authentic person—growing in his understanding of God, self, and other persons—constrained to speak for God in and out of the pulpit.

But the herald of God never parades the dark hours of his soul. He admits to them; he does not advertise them. The "spiritual preoccupations" which delighted the eighteenth-century pietists are not to be confused with existential biblical preaching. The disposition of some contemporary preachers to air their personal doubts and conflicts as an end in itself also obscures God's Word. The pulpit and one's closet prayer room are interdependent; they are not interchangeable.

The content of biblical preaching is the Word itself—the law and the gospel, God's demands and promises. It is the means

[28] Pearson, *The Ministry of Preaching*, pp. 78-79.

whereby Christ himself appeals to persons through the person of the preacher.[29] The Word—heard, accepted, acted on—is the means whereby Christ makes witnesses. The urgency to proclaim God's Word to the ends of the earth is inherent in the message itself. It is the treasure, not the earthen vessel, which provides the constraint and content for saving witness.

Humility. Contemporary man is out of touch with the biblical concept of humility. Political leaders are adored, TV stars are idolized, and military figures are canonized—because they are "so sincere," "so humble." What the Christian sees in this is a cultural fault and an emptiness in persons which combine to equate sincerity and humility with truth. Frank Lloyd Wright is reported to have said that he was forced to decide between being arrogantly self-confident or hypocritically "humble." That is a searing judgment on contemporary culture, as well as on the gifted Mr. Wright.

Contemporary man needs desperately to recover the biblical concept of humility. It is on this order. The humble man, in response to the gospel, wants to surrender his innate disposition to depend on himself and other selves and seeks to act on that desire. The humble man prays as well as plans. He ventures boldly for the sake of God's kingdom, trusting his Lord to use his imperfect witness constructively. The humble man does not venerate the Bible as an object of faith but uses it instead as a means of grace, convinced that God speaks to him now. He is not cavalier about the love which his wife and children bestow on him nor casual about any person's confidence in him. He dares to believe that Christ is inhabiting *his* person, that the Holy Spirit is shaping him along the heroic lines of Christ's person. Claiming God's grace and wrestling with his demands,

[29] Paul Scherer, *For We Have This Treasure* (New York: Harper & Row, 1944), pp. 38-50. This is an invaluable book.

the humble (meek) man inherits the kingdom *and* the earth. Confidence in God, not man, is the core of Christian humility.

But Christian humility is elusive. Paradoxically, no one is in greater danger of succumbing to pride in its subtle forms than the earnest Christian. He needs the redeeming power of Christ in all seasons, and knows it.

Nowhere surely are pride and self-importance and conscious striving after effect more incongruous and unpardonable than in the servant of the Cross. Yet pride would not be the basic sin it is, if it did not possess this demonic quality, that precisely where you would expect to find it lying dead for ever, there it reappears, insinuating itself in even subtler guise. "The final human pretension," Reinhold Niebuhr has reminded us, "is made most successfully under the aegis of a religion which has overcome human pretension in principle." [30]

Christian humility distinguishes between the treasure and the earthen vessel; it does not equate the Light with the lamp.

Hope. Prophetic preaching is demanding, but it is not essentially denunciatory. Its content is law *and* gospel, ethical instruction *and* good news. It sounds the strong note of hope every time. Prophetic preaching comforts (literally "makes strong") because it testifies to the God who raised Jesus from the dead, to the Resurrection Christ, present now, who will come again to establish his Kingdom forever, and to the Holy Spirit who gathers new persons into the new community.

The prophetic view of human life and history provides sustenance and promises fulfillment to those who live in the community of faith: the faltering Christian crying out, "O wretched man that I am"; the despairing thief pleading, "Remember me, Lord"; the onetime wastrel asking, "Make me" instead of "Give me"; the faithful remnant in a totalitarian

---

[30] James S. Stewart, *Heralds of God* (New York: Charles Scribner's Sons, 1946), p. 205.

society pleading, "How long, O Lord?" Because God has acted and continues to act in the human situation, sin has lost its sting, death is swallowed in victory, the Lord wipes away all tears. No human situation can overmatch the Cross. No personal tragedy, however devastating, lies beyond Christ's power to reclaim it. So Paul exults, "The sufferings of this present time are very slight compared with the weight of glory laid up for me." Hope is the dominant note in prophetic preaching.

Summary Statement

The servant of the Word is God's unique creation. None is quite like another nor should he seek to be. Imitation Fosdicks, Marshalls, Scherers, and Thielickes mock God's creative genius. The authentic preacher is a servant of the Word, but he is a unique servant. He is the Holy Spirit's handiwork. Called to be a colaborer with Christ, he places his confidence in the gospel of God *and* in the human activity of preaching. Lack of confidence in either maims the church's exercise of Christ's ministry. God's ambassador views his vocation to preach as actress Julie Harris views her vocation to act—"It is my life!"

Let any ordained minister in Christ's church come before the tribunal of biblical evidence to get his bearings if he does not believe that God was in Christ, that the Scriptures witness to that mighty deed, *and* that preaching is a primary means for communicating this news to man. Treason against one's government is despicable and dangerous. Treason against the kingdom of God—unconfessed and persisted in—destroys the traitor and robs Christ of his appeal.

"Jesus came preaching." His coworkers still do, emboldened by the Holy Spirit to believe that Christ is appealing to the world through them. "The foolishness of preaching" is an elemental tactic in God's overall strategy to save the world.

II

the gospel and human nature

I charge thee in the sight of God and of Christ Jesus who shall judge the living and the dead. . . . Preach the word; be urgent in season, out of season; reprove, rebuke, exhort, with all longsuffering and teaching.

—Paul (II Tim. 4:1-2 ASV)

1

The Prodigal's Father

"The Prodigal's Father" dates back to 1948 when a Marine veteran (World War II), part of the postwar college generation, confronted me, an assistant professor of history at Gettysburg College, with the question, "What is God like? Skip the religious jargon and say it plain." The four thrusts in this sermon emerged from that encounter. The Marine's questions shaped the content and evoked the style. In the course of our friendship, his hard-nosed approach prompted other sermons.

When I accepted the pastorate of College Church (at Gettysburg) during his junior year, the young man stated bluntly that he could trust my witness no longer because I had become "a professional religionist." Nonetheless, the friendship survived, and the dialogue continued. He agreed finally to attend church on an experimental basis. Searching for reality, open to the Word in plain preaching, he became a regular worshiper at College Church, a confirmed member, a rugged evangelist. He established a Christian marriage and serves presently as an officer in a congregation in an eastern city. During his senior year he suggested that our first dialogue (1948) be presented as a sermon. "The Prodigal's Father," conceived in 1948, was born in 1950!

At Trinity Church in 1953 "the Marine's sermon" was preached again in a very different parish situation—a 225-year-old congregation, a central city church, an 800-seat colonial sanctuary less than a third filled. Members of the official board reported that they had to defend the sermon everywhere among the "old guard" who resented its content, thrust, and style. One discovered quickly that board members were uneasy, too. The sermon contributed to the rising dialogue at Trinity in those critical first years of our life together.

The Word in preaching and teaching, concretely and relevantly set forth, always creates dialogue (positive and negative) between the pulpit and the pew. And wherever the Word in preaching and teaching is accepted among parishioners it creates dialogue not only *in* the church but *between* the church and the world. "Dialogue," in the Christian sense, is not a technique; it is an event and an experience. It comes with the recurring event of the Word confronting persons through persons.

A trustee in Trinity, reading this manuscript, requested that "The Prodigal's Father" be preached again. It was—to a thousand new worshipers and several hundred more who had first heard it thirteen years earlier. Some remembered it!

Text—Luke 15:11-32

In the literature of Western society few stories are better known than Jesus' story of the prodigal son. It warms our hearts, stirs our imaginations, captivates our minds, sets our spiritual pulses to pounding. Its poignant theme—rebellion, reconciliation, renewal—strikes a responsive human chord. The truth that any man can go home again is the truth every man needs desperately to hear and act on.

But the "Parable of the Prodigal Son," as it is popularly called, does not claim the son as hero. The central figure in the story is the father. He gave the boy his inheritance, never forgot him, was openhearted when he came home penitently. The prodigal's decision to return home was, in fact, based on the expectation that his father would take him back, if not as a son then as a hired hand. The prodigal's father stands at the center of the parable.

Jesus, telling the story, aimed to reveal *his* Father's heart to man. All four parables recorded in the fifteenth chapter of Luke's Gospel are part of his teaching on the nature of God: the shepherd who seeks a single sheep that has strayed from the fold; the householder who searches indefatigably for one lost coin; the father who banquets a returning prodigal and keeps his home open to a mean-spirited son. If John 3:16 is the "gospel in miniature," as Luther observed, the fifteenth chapter of Luke is a gospel vignette. The parables recorded there provide the fundamentals of Christian theology: man's rebellion against and estrangement from God; the Father's concern for and active seeking of his lost children; every man's freedom to decide; God's abiding joy when a rebel chooses to come home.

In the parable of the prodigal son Jesus points to these characteristics of God.

—God, the willing father of all mankind, accepts the responsibilities inherent in fatherhood; he works to reestablish and maintain his family.

—God loves all people exactly as they are, wherever they are, in whatever condition they are; his redemptive love is claimed on need, not merit.

—God's love brims over with the vigor of his holiness; his demands are inseparable from his promises.

—God saves man without violating human freedom and lifts all who respond to a higher level of freedom; his righteous love transforms rebels into sons.

I

God, the father of all mankind, accepts the responsibilities inherent in fatherhood. He seeks continuously to reestablish and maintain his family. Because of man's rebellion and estrangement, God acted decisively in Christ. The core of Jesus' message is that the Father's home is open, that God wants his wayward children to come home.

Presently, this Christian affirmation draws strong criticism from three secular sources: cultural history, the new sciences of personality, and dialectical materialism. The first argues that Christianity's emphasis on the fatherhood of God is not unique. The second holds that man, bound by infantilism, projects a "cosmic father" as a substitute for his childhood parent. The third, concreted in communist states, rejects all religion as "the opiate of the people." [1]

The uniqueness of Christianity, however, does not rest on the *idea* of God's fatherhood. Christians know that the *idea* itself is not unique. Indeed, a distortion of the idea is lodged in Greek mythology—Zeus, father of the gods! The Christian message rests not on an idea but on objective reality: God's self-revelation in a historical person, Jesus of Nazareth. That is the essence of Christianity's uniqueness: God was in Christ. In him God demonstrated that he is the willing Father, that the Father-child relationship does not rest initially on man's desire but on God's concern for him. Jesus reminded his followers: "You have not chosen me; but I have chosen you." Man loves God because God first loved him.

This magnificent truth comes into sharp focus if it is examined in the setting of the human family. When a child first says, "Father," "Mother," his parents are thrilled. But if the child's parents do not love him enough to accept the responsibilities of parenthood, he lives outside the family circle. The initiative in the parent-child relationship does not rest with the child. Free to reject or accept parental love, a child cannot love his parents meaningfully unless they love him. We come into God's family by adoption. He not only accepts us; he chooses us. We love God because he first loved us.

The notion that man projects the image of a cosmic father also falls before God's revelation of his person in the historical Jesus

[1] See sermon 12, "Can Christianity Overmatch Communism?" pp. 154-65.

who proclaimed that the Father had sent him, and that those who had seen him had also seen the Father. The Christian faith rests on God's progressive self-revelation communicated to man through myth, legend, historical events, persons (prophets), and finally in the historical person of Jesus.

The message and person of Jesus are datable. Christianity accepts the little child of Bethlehem, the man from Nazareth, the persuasive preacher with a Galilean accent, the courageous man on Calvary whom the centurion acknowledged as the Son of God. In the days of Augustus and Herod and Pilate God concreted himself in a human body. Whether one accepts the incarnate God, rejects him, or treats him casually does not alter the reality that he *is* as he revealed himself to be in Christ. That is the ground on which Christians rest their teaching on the fatherhood of God. It is not viewed as an idea to be debated but as a reality to be proclaimed.

The Christian God *is* the willing Father of all mankind, eager to accept the responsibilities inherent in fatherhood and able to meet them creatively. To demonstrate that saving truth inside history, he sent his only Son into the world to persuade wayward children to come home. For this purpose, Jesus, "very God of very God," laid down his life on Calvary. "Greater love hath no man than this." God, the willing Father of all mankind, accepts and fulfills the responsibilities inherent in fatherhood.

II

God loves man in his sin. The prodigal, "living it up" in the far country, his energies spent in riotous living, his mind in bondage to the flesh, forgot his father for a season. But the father did not forget his son.

Every parent experiences something of this at one time or another. Children can get so involved with their own persons and pursue their own ways so egocentrically for a season that they forget their parents. But responsible parents never forget their children. That is another characteristic of Jesus' Father: he loves all men exactly as they are wherever they are, in whatever condition they are. God's love cannot be earned; it is freely given. In the hour of man's most desperate need God is most active in providing rescue. Christ died for us while we were outside the Father's family.

There are evidences of this luminous truth in the Old Testament. The psalmist testifies that, though one makes his bed in hell, God seeks him there, and that no one need walk alone in the valley of death. The book of Jonah, if one frees that reluctant prophet from the whale, witnesses dramatically to God's indefatigable love. God loved the Ninevites in their sin. It was Jonah who could not muster a modicum of love for them. But God kept at Jonah until his dilatory spokesman carried the divine offer of hope and renewal to the wayward Ninevites. They repented. God rejoiced. Jonah sulked. The book of Jonah—frequently abused, often misunderstood, presently unused—packs a hard evangelical wallop!

Another high-water mark in the Old Testament's witness to God's all-embracing love is the book of Hosea. When that ancient man of God came upon his wayward wife, broken and spent by her reckless way of living, he looked on her compassionately, gathered her to himself, took her home, loved her back to wholeness again. That in itself is a poignant story, but there is more. The Holy Spirit led Hosea to see that if he, a man, could love like that, God's love must be much broader and deeper. Constrained by this exciting knowledge, Hosea reminded his contemporaries how, again and again, Israel had gone a-whoring and how God, again and again, had forgiven and loved Israel back to wholeness. In that very hour of Israel's waywardness Hosea preached that God was offering her a clean page, another chance, a fresh beginning.

God's amazing love is revealed most fully, of course, in the person of Christ who shared man's lot from the cradle to the grave, who for our sake and our salvation suffered under Pontius Pilate and was crucified. And his amazing love is focused most sharply in that *Person* on Calvary: "Father, forgive them for they know not what they do."

The staggering truth that God loves all men exactly as they are, wherever they are, in whatever condition they are outflanks the most versatile imagination. It is too big to capture. The best theologies stumble under the weight of it. The most persuasive gospel preaching falls short in proclaiming it. Christian hymnody almost captures it: "There's a wideness in God's mercy like the wideness of the sea"; and again, "To those who fall how kind thou art, how good to those who seek." But Scripture offers the strongest statement: "God so loved the world that he gave." So loved! So loved! That is the dominant theme in the Christian symphony—God so loved—gave—only Son.

The truth that God loves the world in its sin, loves it in spite of its "lostness," is appealing and persuasive. It is also disturbing and disruptive. Many who sing, "There's a wideness in God's mercy" simply do not face up to the worldly implications of God's love. If one is a Republican, he must understand that God loves all the Democrats exactly as they are, including Hubert Humphrey and Wayne Morse. If one is a Democrat, he must get accustomed to the fact that God loves all the Republicans as they are, including Nelson Rockefeller and Barry Goldwater. Americans for Democratic Action must learn that God loves the John Birchers who must, in turn, realize that God loves the ADAers. The WASPs must accommodate to a God who loves the "civil rights" leaders who in turn must accept the authority of a God whose patience is not exhausted by people who think more highly of themselves than they ought to think.[2]

Other examples may strike closer home. If one has a difficult mother-in-law, he may be distressed to learn that God loves her exactly as she is! A plant manager, troubled by workers who decline to give an honest day's work for equitable pay, must accept the fact that God loves them exactly as they are. An employee whose boss is irascible must acknowledge that God loves that boss exactly as he is. The church itself is loathe to recognize that God loves Kosygin and Mao and Franco and Castro exactly as they are. This "new" kind of thinking—hard for mortal man to grasp, harder to accept—prompted Jesus to advise every eager follower to think through the implications of discipleship before pledging his loyalty.

But what hope is there for any *one* of us unless God does love *all* of us exactly as we are? Some church people know the far country of riotous living; all members know the far country of egocentric living. Man's only hope lies with a God who loves each person exactly as he is, wherever he is, in whatever condition he is. Divine grace covers humanity: prodigals and dutiful sons, adulterers and moralists, Communists and capitalists, Democrats and Republicans, Christians and Hindus, Negroes and WASPs. God's grace is man's reason for hope, his source of joy.

III

God's all-inclusive love is not gelatinous. It is structured by his righteousness. The prodigal's father did not forget his son. It is equally true that the father did not prostitute his character nor compromise the integrity of his household to fit the irresponsible

[2] This paragraph in the sermon has been updated.

ways of the prodigal. The father did not say to the son who stayed home, "I miss your brother terribly. Let's move our home halfway to the pigsty and coax him home." He did not compromise, cajole, coerce. The father's house was open to the prodigal because the father's heart was open. But the rebel had to face reality and return on the father's terms. The father-child relationship with the Christian God cannot be established at the expense of God's righteousness.

Currently, some evangelicals emphasize God's promises while ignoring or minimizing his demands. These earnest people insist that God will forgive them because they think that it is God's business to forgive everyone. Like Voltaire, they consider such a god "most useful to mankind." This view is unbiblical. It subverts the gospel. It obscures Christ's revelation of God. It cheapens divine grace. God is not obliged to forgive anyone nor disposed to reject anyone. He is neither an indulgent grandfather nor a cosmic policeman. He is a *righteous* father. He yearns for his wayward children, but they must return on his terms. One cannot have faith without repentance. Gospel faith (justifying faith) and repentance are inseparable. "Cheap grace" does not liberate man for new life in Christ. God's demands and promises comprise his Word to man. The good news and ethical instruction are inseparable.

The prodigal's father loved his son in spite of the boy's pigsty manner of living. But the father did not wink at his son's waywardness, nor excuse the squandered inheritance, nor accommodate his righteous person to the lad's self-centered life. The prodigal could accept his father's love on the father's terms or live outside the healing power of that love. The decision was his to make. Repentance, a continuing act, calls one to turn away from sin, to throw himself on God's mercy, and to do God's commandments. Paul defined this divine-human encounter succinctly: "God was in Christ reconciling the world to himself, . . . [therefore] be reconciled to God" (II Cor. 5:19-20). Apostolic preaching was pointed: Repent. Believe. Come home. Accept your given place in the family of God.

God loves all Republicans and Democrats, liberals and conservatives, Negroes and whites and Puerto Ricans, fringe groups and responsible citizens, murderers and legislators, Communists and capitalists, but each individual among them must accept Christ's commandments if he wants to claim God's love. Whoever lives in the far country of racial prejudice, deaf to Christ's pleas for brotherhood, is estranged from God. Whoever hoards or squanders his inheritance, ignoring the disciplines of Christian stewardship, is in the far country of egocentric living. Whoever looks contemptuously on faltering human beings, insisting arrogantly that one need not shoulder another's burden, is outside the family of God. Those who compromise or ignore God's demands negate his promises.

God loves all people exactly as they are, wherever they are, in whatever condition they are. But any church which allows its members and the world to think that God's grace is cheap serves neither the members nor the world, because it does not serve God. Man must come home on God's terms, for God's sake *and* man's. And that is an issue which every man in his freedom must decide for himself.

IV

God saves willing persons through their freedom, without violating their freedom, lifting them to a higher kind of freedom. Contemporary man needs desperately to face the implications of his "dreadful freedom." On other occasions we have addressed our thinking to this crucial issue, and we shall do so again. But this particular sermon is not a treatise on the freedom of the human will nor an inquiry into the liberty of the Christian man, although both ideas run through it. The sermon addresses itself to the question, "What is God like?"

Consequently, it is enough to recall here that the prodigal asked for his inheritance and that the father gave it. God respects human freedom. Each man, within his historical existence, is free to decide basic personal issues for himself. God does not despoil that freedom. Each is free to waste or use selfishly his time, talent, and material goods. Every man is free to go to hell! Each is equally free to face himself as a rebel, change his irresponsible way of living, and come home. Life with God is open to everyone.

Whoever says, "I will arise and go to my Father"—and does—is welcomed by God himself. The penitent wastrel is not required to cool his heels in the Father's reception hall. He is not subjected to the third degree about the far country. He is not placed on probation. Every prodigal is received as a son. One of the most persuasive lines in Scripture tells that while the prodigal was yet afar off, his father went out to meet him. The father could not contain his joy. The fatted calf was killed; the banquet table was set; the neighbors were called in; merriment rang through the halls.

Until the wastrel acts decisively, however, he cannot claim his rightful place in the family of God. Because God wants sons, he does not employ coercion. A rebel can be expatriated, imprisoned, executed. A slave can be held against his will by superior force. A servant can be held against his desire because he needs money. But a son lives with his father freely and lovingly. The spirit of man is free to attach itself to whom it will. The prodigal's elder brother, unwilling to rejoice with those who rejoiced, demonstrated that man's freedom is indeed a "dreadful freedom" (Luke 15:25-32). God not only waits; he also pleads. Any man can claim his inheritance; God will not withhold it. Any man, lost in the far country of self-centered living, can decide to go home; God will welcome him as a son. On the other hand, each can despise God's promises and ignore his demands choosing to live under his own authority. One thief on Calvary was saved; the other was lost. The issue was decided on the field of human freedom. God saves willing persons through their freedom, without violating their freedom, lifting them to a higher kind of freedom.

God's heart is a father's heart. He loves his children in their waywardness. His love is structured by his righteousness. Wanting sons, he violates no man's freedom, letting every man be free to decide that relationship for himself.

Let us arise and go to our Father.

2

What Do We Mean, "Original Sin"?

Like other sermons preached in the winter and spring of 1954, "What Do We Mean, 'Original Sin'?" was aimed at developing biblical-doctrinal fiber in the congregation. It aroused vigorous response. Some complained that the condition of natural man had been overdrawn. Others suggested that the need for salvation had been understated. The initial exchanges, occasionally heated, turned into a dialogue which centered on the biblical view of man. From there we got into doctrinal theology and secular existentialism. Reinhold Niebuhr's *Nature and Destiny of Man*, D. R. Davies' *Down Peacock's Feathers*, H. Richard Niebuhr's *Christ and Culture*, Paul Tillich's *The Courage to Be*, and Albert Camus' *The Fall* were shared with those who wanted to dig into the question. This ministry of serious reading, described in *From Tradition to Mission*, pp. 97-100, is a strand in parish renewal and a dynamic piece in the ongoing witness of the revived parish.

Years later (Lent, 1965), I preached the sermon again. Stung by some unfair attacks from the community during the 1964 presidential election,[1] I examined freshly the several faces of man which are sharply sketched in Harper Lee's *To Kill a Mockingbird*, James Michener's *Report of the County Chairman*, the Overstreets' *The Strange Tactics of Extremism*, and the "Passion History." Then I rewrote the "old" sermon. The ensuing dialogue focused on the "new morality." Several sessions of "Coffee and Conversation with the Clergy"[2] centered on amorality in politics, love outside marriage, therapeutic abortion, mercy killing, suicide to escape brainwashing, preventative war, the Puritan ethic, etc.

The substance of this sermon comes from an address I delivered

[1] See sermon 13, especially the introductory statement.
[2] See Appendix II.

at an eastern regional meeting of the Lutheran Student Association at Buck Hill Falls, Pennsylvania, in 1950. Attending that conference was a Princeton University student whose home church was Trinity, Lancaster. We did not meet, but from that "encounter" Trinity Church inquired into my ministry when its pulpit became vacant in 1952. The young man's father was on the pulpit committee! Fifteen years later, the "youth," now a college professor, is an active evangelist in Trinity Church. "The wind bloweth where it listeth."

John Crown, hopelessly maimed in World War II, died in a veterans' hospital in New York City after four and a half years of physical pain and mental anguish. A letter which he wrote to a newspaper columnist shortly before his death carried this sobering thrust:

My name is John Crown. My physical wounds are very small in comparison with my spiritual wounds. I have come back from death to a world I no longer care for. . . . All the troubles of the world originate in the common man. . . . When the morals of the common man drop, so do the morals of the nation and of the world. Until each of us stops hogging the road with his car, stops fighting over the seat on the bus, stops arguing over who is going to cut the grass, there will be no peace in the world.

John Crown's poignant letter evidences little awareness of complex sociopolitical realities, the ambiguities which confront those who seek to be Christian in a religionized culture, or the limitations inherent in man himself. Nonetheless, the hard core of his letter reflects reality. Man must pull himself together if he wants to keep his world from being blown to pieces or fragmented by revolutionary forces.

Man's elemental need for acceptance, understanding, and

love has haunted every generation in human history. The early Christians established a beachhead in the Roman world because they out-loved, out-gave, and out-died their pagan contemporaries. Twentieth-century man's hard-pressed search for social and economic justice and his uneven efforts to keep the peace between political power blocs are doomed to failure unless he gets to know his own limitations and is enabled to realize his possibilities.

Presently, man copes with nature better than he copes with human nature. He handles missiles more successfully than he deals with revolutionary forces in Africa and Latin America. He transplants a kidney more readily than he reunifies Germany. He expands the national economy more easily than he extends the frontiers of racial brotherhood. Certainly the human equation is not less significant in building the good society than are socioeconomic forces.

But what can man soberly expect of himself and other men? After all, Scripture insists that man, unredeemed, spoils everything he touches including his own person. That is a bitter pill for many to swallow. Some churchmen, exposed to the doctrine of original sin, respond like Huckleberry Finn: "The statements was interesting, but tough." How errant is man? How radical is the dislocation in human nature? If there is a structural weakness in man can it be corrected? Can the leopard change his spots?

"Man has always been his own most vexing problem." On that note Reinhold Niebuhr launched his influential Gifford Lectures a quarter of a century ago.[3] But one need not be a professional theologian to reach that conclusion! Each has lived long enough with himself and other selves to know firsthand how vexing *any* self can be. Guilty of pettiness on any day, one is apt to say,

[3] *The Nature and Destiny of Man* (New York: Charles Scribner's Sons, 1943), p. 1.

"Do forgive me; I'm not myself today!" It is man's nature to roll in the mud, to stick his nose in his neighbor's business, to cast an envious eye on what belongs to another. Occasionally, however, man turns his face to the sun, adopts a heroic stance, and acts sacrificially. That is human nature, too! "What a chimera then is man, what a novelty, what a monster, what chaos, what a subject of contradiction, what a prodigy! Judge of all things, yet an imbecile earthworm; depository of truth, yet a sewer of uncertainty and error; pride and refuse of the universe." [4]

Man is a house divided against itself. The horse, the dog, the giraffe do not carry a battlefield within. Man alone experiences violent inner civil war. He knows failure and achievement, frustration and satisfaction, misery and grandeur. But he never quite knows what his lot will be.

> Within my earthly temple there's a crowd;
> There's one of us that's humble, one that's proud;
> There's one that's broken-hearted for his sins;
> There's one that unrepentant sits and grins;
> There's one that loves his neighbor as himself,
> And one that cares for nought but fame and pelf.
> From much corroding care I should be free
> If I could once determine which is me.[5]

Like the psalmist we also ask, "What is man that thou art mindful of him?" Is he destined to grandeur or misery? Is man meant to be hero or coward, creator or destroyer, saint or sinner? Which is really he: Churchill or Hitler, Lincoln or Stanton, Francis of Assisi or Attilla the Hun? And what of that

[4] Blaise Pascal, *Pensées*, Louis Lafuma, ed., John Warrington, tr. (New York: E. P. Dutton & Company, 1960), p. 65.
[5] Edward Sandford Martin, "Mixed."

matchless Man from Nazareth? Is his authentic person intended to mock or to awaken hope in mortal man?

"There are resources in the Christian faith for an understanding of human nature which have been lost in modern culture." [6] The idealistic interpretation of man which exalts his rational faculties misunderstands him. Committed to this view, John Stuart Mill argued less than a century ago that man, a reasonable being, would outlaw war in the foreseeable future. Hitler's rape of Poland and the Low Countries, the Nazis' extermination of six million Jews, the Communist purges in Russia, the nuclear arms race, and the vicious bigotry in the United States and South Africa shatter one's unqualified confidence in man's rational faculties. That line from one of A. A. Milne's plays, "If I were God, I'd be very proud of man," has a hollow ring these days.

The awful truth is that man often does the evil which his reason rejects. Mark Antony was willing to let Rome sink in the Tiber as long as he could spend his days with Cleopatra. The 1964 presidential election revealed deep irrationality in both political parties. The "Old South" and the metropolises of the North are less than rational in their addressment to deep-seated racial tensions. For good or ill, the heart has reasons which reason does not understand. If Renaissance man had honored the psalmist's insights into the nature of man, Sigmund Freud might have been an undistinguished Viennese physician! The idealistic view of man distorts reality.

On the other hand the naturalistic interpretation of man fails to appreciate his innate capacity to think, to dream, to create. Man *can* transcend the dimensions of nature. Socrates, Augustine, Michelangelo, Bach, and Lincoln—calling on more than body chemistry and mechanical reflexes—fashioned philos-

[6] Niebuhr, *The Nature and Destiny of Man*, p. 5.

ophy, theology, art, music, and responsible government. Man is more than a bag of chemicals; he is more complex than the Corvette's fuel-injected engine. Biology, chemistry, and physics have contributed greatly to our understanding of man and to the betterment of his physical situation. But the natural sciences fail to explain the man inside the man—that hungering person who cannot live by bread alone.

Why should we suppose that the scientific method of thought—a a method which has been devised for thinking about Inanimate Nature —should be applicable to historical thought, which is a study of living creatures and indeed of human beings? We are sufficiently on our guard against the so-called "Pathetic Fallacy"—of imaginatively endowing inanimate objects with life. We now fall victim to the inverse "Apathetic Fallacy" of treating living creatures as though they were inanimate.[7]

Finally, the existentialist view of man is not a full-fledged interpretation of human nature. It is a corrective in a depersonalized culture. Seeking to recover the individual, existentialism gets bogged down in subjectivism; it offers only partial guidelines. Jean-Paul Sartre, insisting that life is nauseating, offers little hope to man in his essential communal relationships. After all, it is not practical to commit mass hara-kiri! [8]

If the rationalistic and naturalistic (and existentialist) views caricature man and fail to understand him, what contribution does the Christian view make to our understanding of man? The view is on this order.

Human nature has suffered a catastrophe. The unity of man has been broken, his freedom despoiled, by sin. He is a house

[7] Arnold J. Toynbee, *A Study of History,* I (London: Oxford University Press, 1948), 7-8.

[8] The 1965 proclamation of this sermon was followed the next Sunday by one titled, "What Is Christian Existentialism?"

divided against itself. This schism in human nature occurred when man banished God from the citadel of his inner life and set up his ego on a makeshift throne. This rebel government is not able to maintain harmony in any man. Each facet of his personality wars against the other facets. Paul lays that conflict bare: "I do not do the good I want, but the evil I do not want is what I do" (Rom. 7:19). This raging civil war within throws each man into competition and conflict with his fellows, and they with him. The story of the Fall—rescued from liberalism's cavalier attitude toward biblical content and fundamentalism's declination to differentiate form from substance—is myth. It tells how man, having violated his highest freedom by rejecting God's sovereignty, fell into bondage to his own conflicting wants and needs and aspirations, a bondage which he cannot break. Self-will is his natural style of life. Sin is in his blood.

The biblical record testifies to this tragic human condition with unvarnished realism. Consumed with envy, Cain killed his brother in cold blood and then lied to save his own skin. Lust led David to forsake the shepherd of his soul for a season. Pride cost Rehoboam his kingdom. Fear of crossing a new frontier ruined Nicodemus' chance for an authentic life. Cowardice caused Simon Peter to deny his Lord. Envy and bitterness and noninvolvement nailed Jesus to a cross.

Natural man, the Scriptures report matter-of-factly, is in a state of rebellion against God. Consequently, he acts against his own best interests and denies the rights of other persons. Man is saddled with a perverted reason, a dull grey conscience, a will chained to self-interest. Sin, examined before the tribunal of biblical evidence, is an inherited disease beyond human cure, afflicting all alike. Sin and humanness are synonymous. That is the biblical view of natural man.

Will Rogers, when asked "What's wrong with the world

anyway?" drawled, "Well, I dunno, I guess it's people." Some will remember that pungent postwar quip: "How can we have a brave new world with the same old people?" C. G. Jung years ago warned that the evils of primitive man crouch in the recesses of the modern heart.[9] To come upon a group of children who have ganged up on one poor unfortunate playmate whom they torment from sheer perversity is stronger medicine than a "fire and brimstone" sermon! Soldiers from the free world, educated to believe in the doctrine of inevitable progress and reared to view man as essentially good, walked through Dachau and Buchenwald in 1945. Shaken, sobered, nauseated, many questioned and some revised their sanguine views on human nature.

> Three monkeys sat in a cocoanut tree,
> Discussing things as they're said to be.
> Said one to the other, "Now listen you two;
> There's a certain rumor that can't be true
> That man descends from our noble race!
> The very idea's a disgrace.
> No monk ever deserted his wife,
> Starved her babies and ruined her life.
> And you've never known the mother monk
> To leave her babies with others to bunk.
> And another thing you'll never see,
> A monk build a fence around a cocoanut tree,
> And let the cocoanuts go to waste
> Forbidding all other monks a taste.
> Here's another thing a monk won't do;
> Go out at night and get in a stew,
> Or use a gun or club or knife

[9] *Modern Man in Search of a Soul* (Harvest paperback; New York: Harcourt, Brace & World, 1955).

To take another monkey's life.
Yes, man descends ~
The Ornery cuss—
But, brother, he didn't descend from us!" [10]

Every history text records the sins of man. Alexander the Great was vain; Charlemagne was proud; Washington was bad-tempered; Napoleon was arrogant; Lee was provincial; Lloyd George was a philanderer; Wilson was inflexible. The pages of history are crammed with the social consequences of human sin. Carlton J. H. Hayes, onetime professor of European history at Columbia University, is reported to have said that every historian must acknowledge the doctrine of original sin. Whether he acknowledges it or not, the historian records its terrible consequences.

Critical minds are aware that all is not well with man. But they are not agreed on the locus of the trouble, the seriousness of the malady, nor its remedy. Many still cling to one of the twin fictions that man is rational or naturalistic. Consequently, they reason with him or manipulate him. Both approaches lead into blind alleys, produce "confusion roughly organized," breed chaos. The Christian view of man rejects both approaches.

The Lord Christ points up the power of sin. He reveals its depth, tenacity, hatefulness, and death-producing effect. Relentlessly, he tracks it home to the innermost part of man. "It is not that evil befalls us," T. R. Glover observes, "but that we are evil." Natural man is ignorant, wicked, mortal. Face to face with Christ, his deficiencies come frighteningly into focus; and his pretensions are dealt a crushing blow. When Christ confronts man the rebel and demands that conduct and motivation conform to God's holiness, righteousness, and truth, the issue is cleanly defined: Man is not able to meet those demands.

[10] Anonymous.

There is a chasmic difference between excellence and perfection. Education can offer a measure of enlightenment. Psychiatry can break the crust of some neuroses and psychoses. Statesmanship can steady political societies for a season. Only God can rescue man from sin.

Guilt-ridden, searching, puny, man needs pardon, purpose, and power. He needs proper goals, another set of affections, a new life. Man needs a savior. That is precisely why God acted in Christ. Because he loves man, God sent his Son into the world, not to condemn man in his sin, but to save him. Having spoken aforetimes through myth and legend, historical events and persons, the King finally sent his Son on the greatest rescue mission in history. The Son humbled himself and become a man to set the nature and purpose of God before man and to demonstrate authentic humanity. But man was so dead set against God's ways, so bent on his own desires, that rescue cost the life of the rescuer. Jesus died to save man. There was no other way. That is the heart of it—there was no other way.

Many will recall Rudyard Kipling's "If," that jaunty appeal to man to be a *man*. The late Halford Luccock liked to tell how his seminary roommate, who quoted Kipling's poem "If" in sermon after sermon, fared when he preached one night at a Bowery mission on New York's East Side. His friend concluded as usual:

> If you can keep your head when all about you
> Are losing theirs and blaming it on you;
> If you can trust yourself when all men doubt you,
> But make allowance for their doubting too;
>
> . . . .
>
> Yours is the Earth and everything that's in it,
> And—which is more—you'll be a Man, my son! [11]

[11] Used by permission of Mrs. George Bambridge, Doubleday & Company, and the Macmillan Co. of Canada.

Suddenly, a whiskey-soaked voice shattered the spell: "Well, what if you can't?" *That* is the crucial question. What if one can't be a real man in the face of adversity, can't break the encrusted patterns of selfish desire, can't rise above his disposition to honor a status quo which benefits him? What if one can't stand up for truth, speak it plainly, and act on it boldly? What if one can't forgive his enemy, can't do good to those who hurt him, can't find meaning and peace in life? Whoever faces up to this dilemma, wrestles with it, and turns humbly to Christ is on the road to new life. The faith that justifies is alive in him because he is declaring independence from himself by placing his confidence in God.

Paul could declare, "I have run a good race, I have fought a good fight, I have kept the faith," because he faced up to that nagging question, "What if I can't?" and admitted that he could *not*: "I do not do the good I want . . . . O wretched man that I am." Throwing himself on God's mercy, he claimed Christ's victory as his own. Every Christian knows the agonizing tension between the man he naturally is and the Christlike man he yearns to be. Those who allow the gospel to stir this inner tension and who cultivate it by daring to want what Christ wants are delivered from their bondage to sin. They still sin but their love of sinning is gone, and their burden of guilt is lifted as they are drawn closer to Christ. Through faith they become convinced that the imperfect *can* become perfect, that unrighteousness *can* be crowded out by righteousness, that death *can* be overmatched by life.

Sin despoils man's motives, warps his best-intentioned deeds, lures him into blind alleys. But that is not the destiny God planned for him. Man is created for life with God and his fellows. Since Christ won that massive victory over sin, there is imperishable hope for prodigals and elder brothers, Magdalenes and Simon Peters, respectable citizens and religious activists. Christ overmatched man's sin on Calvary. He did for humanity what no man can do for himself or for others.

The Christian pilgrim, acknowledging that he sins in grievous ways which he cannot fully understand, remembers gladly that his rebellion is forgiven, that he can go home again, that he can be a co-heir with Christ. He acts boldly on that!

3

Why Must People Suffer?

Every parish pastor is obliged to tackle this thorny question again and again. He does so because his parishioners ask it, because he asks it in their behalf as he participates in their suffering, and because the suffering of Jesus constrains him. He also asks the question in behalf of his loved ones and himself from time to time, especially when they and he experience rejection as they seek to witness to God's Word which sears before it heals.

"Why Must People Suffer?" is a sermon which, like Topsy, grew across the years. Its structure, however, is the same as it was when it was first preached in 1955: suffering is punitive, remedial, redemptive, mysterious. It opened a number of pastoral conversations and precipitated fourteen new pastoral counseling situations. The punitive aspect of suffering prompted five persons to seek help (guilt). The remedial aspect intrigued three. Five came to explore "the margins of mystery" around human suffering, notably their own. One came because the redemptive aspect of suffering challenged him.

Across the years a dozen or so sermons have been preached in Trinity on the subject of suffering—"The Margins of Mystery," "Christ's Suffering and Ours," "Christ and Job on Suffering." The emphases in "Why Must People Suffer?" were reexamined in 1959 when some parishioners who had attended the Broadway play, *J.B.*, asked that Archibald MacLeish's drama be evaluated. The substance of this sermon appeared in a collection of Lenten sermons, *Preaching the Passion* (Philadelphia: Fortress Press, 1963), and is included here with permission.

"I have said this to you, that in me you may have peace. In the world you have tribulation; but be of good cheer, I have overcome the world." (John 16:33.)

Often in the course of contemporary preaching it is necessary to demonstrate that a particular problem exists before one can let the gospel illuminate it and from its resources help people cope with it creatively. But when the subject is human suffering, the preacher can tackle the problem with few preliminaries. To live is to suffer sometime, somewhere. Jesus accepted that reality: "In the world you have tribulation." Paul also exhorted his coworkers to accept their "share of hardship."

Suffering is not always evident to the passerby. Some people, cruelly used, decline to speak of their suffering. Robert Louis Stevenson was like that. In spite of mounting pain he cultivated a gay spirit in a deteriorating body. Helen Keller made the world forget that life had shortchanged her. Lincoln, burdened by the nation's trial by fire, was remarkably restrained in speaking of his personal and vicarious suffering. Jesus met his crucifixion so gallantly that a hard-bitten Roman centurion at Calvary declared, "This was the Son of God."

On the other hand, there are kinds and degrees of suffering which cannot be hidden. They parade in full dress for all the world to see: the Battle of Britain, the Dresden fire raid, Hiroshima under the "mushroom cloud." Cancer, a death in the family, poverty—each inflicts a kind of suffering which squats on one's front porch. The world's doorstep is crowded with suffering: starving people in Asia and Africa; manipulated, exploited, persecuted persons in every nation; humanity living in dread of a nuclear holocaust. All too often, suffering is a public spectacle.

Whether one suffers secretly or openly, everyone gets his share of hardship. No one is slighted. No vaccine protects against it. No alcoholic escapade banishes it. No religious charm prevents it. Suffering has more roots than a poplar tree. It comes with physical illness and accident. It comes in the wake of personal failure. It is spawned by war. It is part of one's growing knowledge of his own imperfect person and his disappointing experience with other imperfect persons. Suffering is an integral part of life. Since the gospel of God sheds light on all the facets of life, we turn to it eagerly.

I

The gospel enables us to accept the awful truth that suffering is often punitive. It is the consequence of man's abuse of his freedom. Jesus did not mince words: "What a man sows, he also reaps"—of evil as well as of good. Mental anguish, for example, can be the consequence of a loose tongue. Physical suffering can be caused by overindulgence, unbroken tension, burning the candle at both ends. Spiritual suffering in the guise of nostalgia and frustration in middle life can be the consequence of undisciplined intellectual and emotional living in one's formative years: "For of all sad words of tongue or pen, the saddest are these: 'It might have been!' " [1] Not all suffering is shrouded in mystery. Wave after wave rolls in as undisciplined lives collide with the physical and moral laws of God's universe. Every man should confess, "I have sinned against thee, O God, in thought, word, and deed." Each should cry, *mea culpa.*

But guilt is not only personal; it is also corporate. If one argues simply that the Nazi war criminals "got what was coming to them" at the Nürnberg trials, can he really dismiss the Nazi horror so summarily? Himmler, Goebbels, Göring, and their colleagues did not accomplish those atrocious crimes against humanity in a social vacuum. What guilt must the German generals and industrialists bear for accepting Hitler in the early 1930's? What guilt must the German citizenry accept for ignoring the "confessing church" in the mid-1930's and for taking pride later in Hitler's "blitzkrieg war," 1939 and 1940?

[1] John Greenleaf Whittier, "Maud Muller."

What measure of guilt rests with England and France for the punitive Versailles Treaty and with all the Western democracies for isolating the hard-pressed Weimar Republic? Guilt is corporate because it is personal.

America, ill-prepared for World War II and badly frightened because its naval power had been reduced severely by Japan's powerful onslaught at Pearl Harbor, was quick to make General Short and Admiral Kimmel the scapegoats for the December 7, 1941, debacle. In due season, however, most Americans attached degrees of blame to the President of the United States, the State Department, the America First Committee, and finally to themselves for preferring illusion to reality during those two eventful decades after World War I. Guilt is corporate. "Like sheep, we have all gone astray."

To live is to be caught up inextricably in the web of human association. No man is an island unto himself. Sin is infectious; its consequences range far and wide, often to the third and fourth generation. No individual or group or nation comes before God with clean hands. Only Christ can say, "Which of you accuseth me of sin?" He alone is free from *all* sins of omission and commission. Saul Kane, lamenting the pain he had caused by being himself, is humanity's honest spokesman. Every man should strive diligently to alleviate some suffering in the world. Each helped fashion it by being so like himself, so unlike Christ! Suffering results when man abuses his freedom. Suffering is punitive.

II

The gospel also teaches that suffering is remedial. This view is presented unforgettably in the book of Job. A critical reading of that matchless drama brings one face to face with the remedial possibilities in suffering. The New Testament does not obscure that view. Actually, it expands and deepens it. Jesus pointed out that new life is not based on a mechanical system of rewards and punishments. He demonstrated that it roots in one's maturing relationship with the living God. Christianity does not produce people who behave like Pavlov's conditioned dogs, Clyde Beatty's dutiful lions, or Marineland's trained porpoises. Christianity calls men to authentic personhood. It is not an ethical system, nor a philosophy, nor a set of dogmas. Christianity is life—life with God and those who serve him. It is life lived by faith in Christ. In that dynamic relationship God refashions uncouth humans after the pattern of Christ's authentic person. Remedial suffering is part of that reshaping process.

If man is placed in this world for the thrilling purpose of maturing into the kind of person who loves freely and witnesses gladly without concern for reward or recognition, the remedial aspect of suffering makes sense. If man is set in the human situation to learn how to live comfortably with God forever, remedial suffering is essential to that dynamic process. George Eliot, no stranger to suffering, wrote, "It would be a poor result of all our anguish and wrestling if we won nothing but our old selves at the end of it." Job in adversity was closer to God than Job in prosperity: "Though he slay me yet will I trust him." Suffering *can* be remedial. In an affluent society where many value comfort above character and honor convenience above conscience, remedial suffering makes sense to those who believe in the God who calls them to authentic personhood.

Mature parents do not shield their children from pain if the experience of it promises to be remedial. Parental hearts bleed when children suffer, but those parents who care more for the character of their offspring than for their own sensibilities will exercise painful disciplines. They subscribe to pain with purpose. They allow to each child a share of hardship because they love their children more wisely than any child loves himself.

Jesus, pointing to this splendid human experience, taught that God, the perfect Father, is immeasurably more able to accomplish good through discipline than any parent; that he allows and employs pain in reshaping persons.

Remedial suffering results whenever God prods individuals to face reality, use their inner resources, and strengthen their relationship with him. Because God loves each person more wisely than any person can love himself or any other person, he employs suffering for remedial purposes.

III

The gospel of God also teaches that suffering, accepted for Christ's sake, is redemptive. Jesus stated categorically that any man's inheritance of the Kingdom hinges on his willingness to follow him into the world and on to Calvary. He wanted it understood—and still does—that taking one's place in his company is a costly venture: "Can you drink of my cup?" Paul, speaking from experience, taught that only those who suffer with Christ will share in his victory. Redemptive suffering is always voluntary. Each man must take up the cross for himself. The fellowship of Christian suffering is not a reluctant corps of conscripts nor a cowed band of galley slaves. It is a company of volunteers.

A reminder on what constitutes a *Christian* cross may be helpful. Men in their freedom choose to suffer for many causes. Lenin suffered for a class. Gandhi suffered for a people. Churchill suffered for his hardy Britons and a free way of life. The suffering of each man generated far-reaching power. None, however, was seeking *primarily* to do God's will. Lenin wanted to "free" the working men of the world. Gandhi sought to free the Indian people from colonialism. Churchill challenged the British to live their "finest hour." Each man put *his* goal above every other consideration. Jesus, on the other hand, suffered as a direct consequence of doing God's will. He entered fully into God's purpose to redeem the *world*. He offered new life to *all* people—not a single class, nor one nation, nor a lone generation. Cross-bearing in the Christian sense involves one in suffering for persons beyond class, caste, and race. It acknowledges no national boundaries and outruns the present moment of history.

Ordinarily, the care one provides for an aged parent is not a cross; it is the enactment of a moral duty. Pagans also care for aging parents. Daily work to maintain one's household is not a cross; it is the fulfillment of one requirement inherent in marriage and family living. Unbelievers also keep that promise. Personal and social suffering which results from one's abuse of freedom is not a cross; it is punishment. "Though the mills of God grind slowly, yet they grind exceeding small." [2] Remedial suffering is not a cross; it is God's righteous love reshaping one's person. The Lord chastens whom he loves. Cross-bearing is voluntary suffering for Christ's sake. It is indispensable to God's ongoing work of redemption.

But redemptive suffering can be sidestepped in our religionized society. Actually, unconverted church members prefer "Christians" who avoid controversial issues and evade costly service to their Lord. Human admonitions to caution—"Don't get involved"; "Don't volunteer"; "Don't rock the boat"—are heard too often in many parishes. Jesus' searing question, "Why call ye me Lord, Lord, and do not my commandments?" is heard politely but heeded rarely.

Jesus could have bypassed Calvary. His closest friends, especially Peter, urged him to avoid Jerusalem. Jesus called Peter a devil for that bit of counsel. Pilate—haunted by his sense of Roman justice, his concern for public order, and his wife's agitated warnings—wanted Jesus to adopt a saner course. Jesus

[2] Friedrich von Logau, "Retribution," tr. by Henry Wadsworth Longfellow.

declined to bargain with Pilate. The Son of God was not compelled to die. He *decided* that for himsef: "No man takes my life from me." He chose to do God's will, to suffer for man's sin, to pioneer a new path for man. That is redemptive suffering.

Albert Schweitzer *decided* to give up his pleasant academic life, study medicine, and sail for equatorial Africa as a medical missionary. Kagawa *chose* to live in Yokohama's slums, accepting poverty, physical injury, and disease for Christ's sake in that inhospitable setting. Dietrich Bonhoeffer *elected* to return to Nazi Germany in 1939 rather than accept a teaching position in the United States. Schweitzer, Kagawa, and Bonhoeffer acted in freedom for *Christ's sake*. To bear his cross is a decision which each man must make for himself.

Neither the law of the land nor membership in this church forces anyone to pray for his enemies, to do good to those who wound him, to give beyond his means, to die for Christ should one's historical situation require *that* as the cost of discipleship. The gospel invites; it does not compel. Whoever accepts Christ as Lord is persuaded and empowered to accept costly discipleship. Everyone who accepts Christ takes up the cross and follows him into the world. Like his Master, the cross-bearer is ignored, rejected, attacked, killed; he is also heard, accepted, honored, followed. Stephen persuaded Paul; Monica influenced Augustine; Wesley fashioned a vigorous evangelical church; Bonhoeffer challenged Christians everywhere.

The gospel of God points to three dimensions of human suffering. It is punitive, remedial, redemptive. Punitive suffering rolls into life like an angry sea when any man, abusing his freedom, acts against God's sovereign will. Remedial suffering slips into life whenever it serves God's purposes in fashioning authentic persons. Redemptive suffering transforms life whenever anyone chooses to follow Christ into the world. The acceptance and application of these biblical insights are sobering, enlightening, encouraging. When one's share of hardship comes he has the gospel to illuminate his way. But every sufferer needs more than light. He needs someone who cares and understands and shares his suffering.

Suffering breeds loneliness and causes isolation. Unshared, it can destroy one's person. Every sufferer needs a Friend who understands him and his predicament. To be truly understood is a strengthening experience. When the pianist, Greig, composed the musical score for Ibsen's poem, "Peer Gynt," Ibsen, hearing the score for the first time, gripped Greig's hand and whispered, "Understood! Understood!" Christ, the High Priest touched by all our infirmities, understands our suffering.

Thomas Carlyle speaks of the philosopher who, looking from an attic window in Paris, brooded over the pain which engulfed that dazzling city. But Carlyle's philosopher was above it all. He was a spectator. The Lord Christ not only looks solicitously on everyman's suffering, he also inquires into it. Indeed, he becomes a participant. Physical pain, mental anguish, dark nights of the soul were part of his experience in this world. His scars allow him to claim first place in the fellowship of suffering. Like other mortals, he wearied, wept, thirsted, hungered, bled, died. But unlike other mortals, he conquered suffering and death. Christ not only understands human suffering; he enters into it. Most significantly, he empowers the sufferer to handle hardship creatively.

The margins of mystery which swirl around human suffering are not completely dispelled by gospel faith. Earthbound, we mortals see through the glass darkly; we cannot understand fully until we meet Christ face to face. But we do not wait in total darkness. The gospel sheds light on human suffering: it is punitive, remedial, redemptive. And beyond this splendid light the gospel calls us into the fellowship of Christ who understands us and our human situation and who gives us the victory.

4

Does Prayer Make Any Difference?

Within six months of coming to "Old Trinity," I was sobered by the sectarian and religious-secular minds of the congregation. During those early years of our life together, both minds resisted the gospel vigorously. Biblicism and anti-intellectualism roamed in every corner of the parish, dominating the church school and the auxiliaries and infecting vestrymen, too. Both minds treated Jesus respectfully, viewed the Bible as an object of faith, and fostered the sharp cleavage between "religion" and "life." This sermon, "Does Prayer Make Any Difference?" was one in a series on "The Bible and the Word of God." The series, preached at intervals, 1954-1956, was conceived as a frontal attack on both minds. It stirred wide response in "Old Trinity."

On the negative side, a substantial bloc of older members insisted that the preacher despised the "sweet hour of prayer," that his preaching was "too intellectual," that he did not "believe in the Bible," that he was "undermining our faith." Several lay leaders were especially active in their phone campaign against the "new" preaching in Trinity. Perhaps a hundred members joined them openly and covertly. Others, however, listened to the criticisms and, their interest awakened, began attending church "to see what was going on down there." Many remained to worship and witness. The Word of the Lord *is* quick and powerful to save!

Actually, a handful of regular worshipers were captivated immediately by the "new" preaching in Trinity. Their eager interest and mounting support fostered dialogue in the parish and the community. This sermon created counseling appointments, strengthened vestry support, and won new members to Trinity. The mimeographed sermon, claimed by friend and foe, was shared and discussed in the community. Two years later we were still receiving an occasional new member through the dialogue prompted by this sermon. It has been preached in college and university chapels and at the annual Pastors' Institute at Princeton Theological Seminary.

James identified one cause of man's trouble, personal and social, when he said, "Ye have not, because ye ask not" (4:2 KJV). Paul, shepherding the young church, urged his fellow pilgrims "to pray without ceasing." James reminded them that the prayers of "a righteous man" are effective.

Jesus himself relied heavily on prayer. Often as the Judean sun sank across the western hills, he would kneel in some secluded place; and as the sun rose the next morning across the land of Moab, he would rise from his all-night rendezvous with God. Jesus prayed on every occasion: at his baptism, when he faced temptation, before choosing his disciples, before performing a miracle. He prayed for little children, the sick, the dying, his disciples, his family, his enemies. Jesus prayed in people's homes, on the road, in the fields, in the marketplace, on the Sea of Galilee, in the synagogue, and in the temple. Faced with Calvary, he retired to Gethsemane to pray. His conviction renewed and his resolve strengthened, he accepted the Cross. His last breath on Calvary was not a moral pronouncement but a prayer: "Father, into thy hands I commit my spirit" (Luke 23:46).

The world cannot measure its debt to those who have closeted themselves with God in expectant prayer. John Knox, Protestantism's bold witness in seventeenth-century Scotland, was a diligent practitioner of prayer. He impressed the Roman Catholic queen, Mary, who feared John Knox's prayers more than an army of ten thousand men. In an especially dark hour of the Civil War, President Lincoln invited the Congregational preacher, Henry Ward Beecher, to remain one evening after the other White House guests had departed; he wanted Beecher to join him in prayer for the broken Union. The renewal of this parish and its rising witness owe incalculably much to intercessory and petitionary prayer. Prayer opens the shutters of man's dark life and lets in the light of God. Prayer channels divine pardon, peace, and power into man's erring, strife-ridden, fragmented existence. Prayer is a lifeline of Christian faith.

Nonetheless, postmodern man neglects prayer shamelessly. Preoccupied with his plans, wearied by a welter of activities, his energies depleted, he simply does not practice the discipline of prayer. Rather than ask the Lord to share his burdens, he throws them over his shoulder and resolutely pushes his own way. Faltering under the mounting weight of those burdens he then insists petulantly that a mate, parent, or political leader must assume them for him.

If Western society turns rarely to prayer, the church itself evidences little commitment to it. In this generation the Christian community speaks diffidently about the power of prayer. It simply is not in style these days. It is a lost art. Most churchmen—when they speak of prayer at all—claim either too *much* for prayer or too *little*. One camp makes sweeping claims which neither the New Testament nor their Christian experience can support. Refusing to examine prayer in the light of God's nature and man's, these insecure believers exaggerate the power of prayer. They offend critical minds which recognize that prayer *is* limited by God's righteousness and majesty and love. He cannot do evil; he will not run errands; he declines to give man hurtful things. Critical minds are also aware that additional limitations are placed on prayer by man's ignorance, wickedness, and mortality. Natural man cannot apprehend, much less comprehend, truth in its totality; his cleanest motives have base strands; he is bound to *his* moment in time. The power of prayer is limited by the nature of God and human freedom. Those who make unqualified claims for prayer caricature the gospel, distort Christian doctrine, and offend critical minds.

On the other hand, many church members claim too little for prayer. Conditioned by mass secular education, intimidated by the technological accomplishments of modern science, and preoccupied with the mechanics of physical existence, these busy church people relegate prayer to a minor place in their daily quest for bread, security, and love. They do not pray in any disciplined fashion for mate, children, parents, church, community, or world. Neither do they pray for themselves except under extreme duress, often to discover then that they do not know how to go about it. Presently, many Christians claim too little for prayer, insulating themselves against its effective power. James speaks acutely to this generation of churchmen: "Ye have not, because ye ask not." There is no excuse for empty lives!

Seeking to steer a course between extreme views, we propose to define three broad areas in which prayer does make a difference. Each worshiper, according to his intimate needs, can fill in the outline of this sermon for himself.

I

Prayer makes a difference in the natural world. The "new sciences" are not shackled by the mechanical world view which Descartes, Newton, and LaPlace bequeathed. The "new physics" has opened many minds to the inherent uncertainties of nature. "In the garbled lexicon of quantum physics," as one scientist put it, "there is no such word as really." Neither the philosophical nor the theological implications of the "new physics" have been plumbed, but both disciplines enjoy a new intellectual climate, more hospitable than the one which prevailed until a generation ago.

Sixty years ago, when Alexis Carrel declared that a dying tubercular patient considered beyond the reach of medical science was cured by prayer, he angered medical doctors on both sides of the Atlantic. The consensus was that Dr. Carrel's report was "unscientific." [1] The intellectual climate has changed radically during the last half century. Presently, trained minds are less doctrinaire and more disposed to admit openly to the margins of mystery. Today the medical profession, accomplishing open heart surgery and kidney transplants, admits to the need to treat the whole man. Competent doctors, alert to the limitations inherent in their specialized scientific disciplines, do not view medical science as an absolute science. They are not as "materialistic" about the physical ills of man as they were a few decades ago. Today, physicians realize that a weakness in any one of the four factors of health—physical, mental, spiritual, social—can and does affect the whole man adversely, militating toward illness.

We are certainly not implying that the mind constitutes the only reality. A delightful limerick which puts that view into proper perspective goes like this:

> There was a faith-healer of Deal
> Who said, "Although pain isn't real,
> When I sit on a pin,
> And it punctures my skin,
> I dislike what I fancy I feel."

---

[1] Alexis Carrel, *The Voyage to Lourdes* (New York: Harper & Row, 1950). See especially the preface by Charles A. Lindberg, pp. 5-8. Also Carrel, *Man, the Unknown* (New York: Harper & Brothers, 1935), pp. 147-50.

The mind and the body are inextricably bound together. Neither can say to the other, "I have no need of thee!" Man is a whole being.

Nor are we suggesting that the laws of nature are capricious. They are quite dependable. The law of gravitation, for example, operates inexorably within a definable space round the earth. If a Boeing 707 Jetliner over the Atlantic loses power in all four engines, the passengers and crew must ditch. If a man, fed up with life, jumps from the Empire State Building only to experience a change of heart at the fourteenth floor, no urgent prayer will arrest his descent. If the foundation of the "leaning tower of Pisa" is weakened sufficiently, Italy will lose a prime tourist attraction.

This is God's world, and God is not capricious. The sun rises and sets. The tides ebb and flow. The seasons change. Prayer is practiced inside a dependable universe which is under God's active control. The universe exists for man who in turn exists to glorify God by growing into Christ's likeness. Consequently, whatever serves God's purpose in reshaping persons is what God does in this world. His thoughts are not our thoughts, and his ways are beyond our finding out. In Christ we are assured that he allows nothing of permanent harm or injury to befall those who commit themselves to his care.

No one who prays persistently in the name of Christ ever comes away empty-handed. God's purpose is always accomplished in, through, and/or for the petitioner. Paul received the power to accept his physical disability and transmute it into a positive good. E. Stanley Jones, on the other hand, received the health he prayed for. He was enabled to engage in God's work for a half century. Prayer makes a difference in the natural world according to God's gracious purposes and man's disciplined practice of it in Christ's name.

II

Prayer makes a difference in how one handles the inevitable situational tensions in life. Internal and external tensions, challenge and response, achievement and failure, are conditions of human freedom. The more responsibilities one assumes, the more new ventures he attempts, the more fresh trails he blazes, so much more severe are his situational tensions. High political office, for example, is viewed enviously by some citizens who have little appreciation of the massive situational tensions attached to it. George Washington fretted constantly under the situational tensions inherent in the Presidency. Lincoln matured under them. Woodrow Wilson faltered under them. But one need not be elected or appointed to high office to face situational tension. All that is required is that one be born! From the cradle to the grave man must cope with situational tension. Learning to walk, getting an education, earning a living, getting married and rearing a family, undergoing surgery, driving an automobile, facing death—every life experience has built-in tension and creates new waves of tension.

Some people resolve these tensions by going to pieces—literally. That eliminates tension for them. It also insulates them against the joy of living. Concerned citizens in every community develop and employ the best medical, psychological, and religious resources to help these disabled people. Most persons, however, do not go to pieces. They seek instead to ease tensions by accepting majority opinion and accommodating to local mores. They go along to get along. An alarming number of people in this generation seek to escape tension by taking a seat on the sidelines of life. They choose to be spectators. These efforts to resolve tension do bring a modicum of immediate relief. In the long run, however, they cause severe, deep-seated anxiety (*angst*). God fashioned human beings to decide, to participate, *to live*. Christ came that man might have abundant life.

When a majority of people decline to participate responsibly in society—seeking to escape life's situational tensions—the foundational social institutions (family, church, school, state) shatter. That is how Rome fell. Fortunately, many people in this generation do face up to life's situational tensions. Some handle them courageously and constructively. Many who handle them creatively testify that their insights and staying power can be traced to a closet prayer room.

Prayer helped Mr. Lincoln cope creatively not only with the terrible situational tensions engendered by the Civil War but also with intimate personal tensions. Mr. Lincoln, perceptive and sensitive, was subject to seasons of deep melancholia. His wife, Mary Todd, had her family roots in the South. His favorite son, Tad, died during the family's residence in Washington. The President worked with several Cabinet members who were constantly at cross-purposes with his aims. Many Northerners, interested only in the abolition of slavery, collided with Mr. Lincoln who worked primarily to save the Union. In 1864 it appeared to Mr. Lincoln that he would not be reelected. A bitterly fought campaign barely returned him to office. As the South crumbled and the Union was preserved, he turned his talents to binding up the nation's wounds. Mr. Lincoln, by his own admission, relied heavily on prayer as he coped creatively with massive situational tensions.

Recall how Judge Harold Medina handled the onerous situational tensions which threatened to engulf him when he presided over the now famous trial of a dozen Communists in the federal court in New York City a decade and a half ago. The tensions inherent in that trial, especially for the presiding judge who was required to keep an impartial court, would have broken some judges and bent most. But Harold Medina, evidencing magnificent self-discipline, presided over the controversial trial so competently that his name is inscribed in legal history. A free society's confidence in "due process of law" was demonstrated to a skeptical world. After the trial Judge Medina stated publicly that his practice of daily prayer and his disciplined worship patterns—which he said had shaped his lifelong reliance on God—kept him from breaking.

Is Harold Medina's testimony essentially different from Paul's: "I can do all things through Christ who strengthens me"? James said, "Ye have not, because ye ask not." If one knows *how* to pray, and if one *does* pray, he is not spared situational tensions. He is equipped to face and handle those tensions constructively.

III

Prayer makes a significant difference in the strengthening of one's desire to integrate his fragmented person. It prods, enlightens, and sustains him in this crucial venture. Prayer helps him identify the warring selves within and bring them under God's authority. It enables him to wrestle steadfastly against partial selves so that a whole self can emerge. Until this inner civil war is quelled, man's potential for constructive action is curtailed sharply, and in some cases shaped to demoniac purposes. That is not God's intention for any man.

God made man for fellowship with him. The creature, therefore, is restless, confused, and lost until he brings his desires, decisions, and deeds into conformity with his Creator's will. Until one establishes the home God approves, engages in the vocation which God endorses, and looks compassionately beyond his own "tight little island" of self-interest, he has not claimed his given place in God's community. But that pilgrimage requires long hours in anguished prayer.

There are, to be sure, "sweet hours of prayer." One cannot live joyously without them. Equally, there are desperate, lonely hours of prayer. One cannot become an authentic person without them. Until Gethsemane gets into one's prayer experience—that titantic struggle between one's stubborn self-will and God's will—authentic personhood cannot break through. Until a man goes to *his* Gethsemane to wrestle with *his* pride, *his* ignorance, *his* greed, *his* lust, *his* envy, *his* cowardice, *his* prejudice, God cannot set him free. "Ye have not, because ye ask not."

There in Gethsemane, alone with Christ, one faces reality. The gray areas of his life are coal black when viewed in the light of Jesus' luminous person. Robert Burns' plea,

> Oh wad some power the giftie gie us
> To see oursels as others see us! [2]

is forgotten as one begins to see himself as God sees him. Those seasons in anguished prayer bring God and man face to face. Any man can flee the righteous God or stay to be refashioned; Gethsemane is where he stays. Naturally, every man's Gethsemane is in the world: an executive's desk, an atomic scientist's conference with the leaders of state, a kitchen sink, a classroom. The Gethsemane prayer occurs wherever one no longer tries to flee the holy God but stays to accept God's will as his own.

Psychiatry liberates some people from their emotional prisons. It also helps many achieve a sane adjustment to life. But only God can fashion authentic personhood. That is precisely what he does for those who go to dark Gethsemane seeking to bring their ways into conformity with his ways. That kind of prayer is lonely, anguished, smells of sweat. It is the hardest work any man can do in this life. But it is essential if one wants authentic personhood. Prayer, linked with worship and the study of the

[2] "To a Louse."

living Word and the daily doing of Christ's commandments, makes the difference between living and existing.

Because the universe exists as an act of God's sovereign will, the more diligently one prays about adjustment and change the better he knows God. Because human history exists to make God's *saving* will known in Christ, the more steadily one prays in the face of situational tensions (daily work, marriage, the threat of nuclear war) the better he trusts Christ. Because each individual is an act of God's creative love, the more courageously one faces himself in the presence of Christ the better habitation he becomes for God's own Son.

Prayer makes a difference in the course of natural events, in handling life's situational tensions, and in enabling one to become an authentic person.

> O what peace we often forfeit,
> O what needless pain we bear,
> All because we do not carry
> Everything to God in prayer! [3]

[3] Joseph Scriven.

5

A Race to Be Run!

"A Race to Be Run," preached in 1965, sought to encourage and challenge the born-again congregation to grow steadily in its rising witness. Addressed particularly to hundreds of parishioners who had come through the hard years of renewal, it asked them to keep alert to spiritual complacency and weariness in well-doing. It challenged newer members to lengthen and quicken their strides. It aimed to jar those who have declined to run at all, preferring to be spectators. It speaks from the gospel to persons at all levels of Christian experience, including teenagers who have not completed the first lap of their Christian race.

This sermon, preached back-to-back with another titled, "The Gospel and Agent 007" (Youth Sunday), found Trinity's three hundred teenagers in my mind's eye. Our teenage son was invited to read the sermon and make suggestions. After several of his observations had streamlined it considerably and framed its introduction, he gave his approval. The coveted teenage "nihil obstat" in our household is, "Not bad, Dad!"

The sermon is an example of noncomplex pastoral preaching. It is quite within the reach of any ordained or *lay* preacher-teacher who studies the Bible, digs into a good commentary or two, and sees himself standing in the tradition of Peter and John Mark who experienced failure before they witnessed effectively. Three laymen in Trinity have preached at the Sunday and Friday noon services. Many are competent teachers, evangelists, and discussion leaders. Several are invited frequently to speak and preach not only in Lancaster but also in other communities.

God committed his Word to the church. It is the church, therefore, which is called to proclaim the good news. Functionally, the pulpit is the focal point for proclamation, but it is not the only place for proclamation. Increasingly, Trinity Church is preaching.

Healthy persons strive to achieve goals. They like to pit their talents and energies against problems and obstacles. Consequently, they enjoy participating in or watching a good race. Some like horse-racing at Pimlico, a few too well! Others appreciate the Penn relays and the Olympic games. A few are frustrated because they never have had their chance at auto racing at Indianapolis or Daytona or the Grand Prix.

The apostle Paul also loved a good race. This is what he wrote to the little church at Philippi. "Brethren, I count not myself to have apprehended: but this one thing I do, forgetting those things which are behind, and reaching forth unto those things which are before, I press toward the mark for the prize of the high calling of God in Christ Jesus." (3:13-14 KJV.)

The citizens of Philippi crowded their city stadium for all the sporting events. Paul had observed how eagerly they watched the runners straining nerve and sinew to be the first to touch the pole at the end of the course. He had sensed how the crowd shared vicariously in the victor's acceptance of a garland of pine, the symbol of victory, from the city's ruler. Writing to the hard-pressed Christians at Philippi, Paul presented himself as a Christian runner on the racecourse of life, straining to win and be called before the Ruler of heaven and earth for commendation. "I have not yet won this race," the Apostle declared. "But forgetting yesterday's victories and defeats, I keep an unbroken stride. Conscious of my uncrowned status, I run to receive the precious prize of unbroken fellowship with God." Consider Paul's directives for receiving that prize. As practical as roast beef and mashed potatoes, the directives are equally useful to teenager and octogenarian.

I

First, a good beginning does not guarantee victory. "I count myself not [yet] to have apprehended." Paul faced the fact that the Christian race is long and arduous: "I have not arrived; I am not yet good enough." He remembered how Jesus had counseled against following him lackadaisically. This hard-eyed recognition that the Christian race is not won in the first several laps is a basic requirement for Christian victory.

Paul might have declared proudly, even petulantly: "I've come a long way since my new-life experience on the Damascus Road. I have outdistanced all the runners of my generation. My labors are more abundant than those of Peter or John." Paul could have made that judgment as a statement of fact. He could have decided to take a "breather" until the others caught up. Several of his letters betray that he occasionally felt like that. His performance proves that he did not give in to his feelings.

Paul could also have decided to rest for a season because he was close to exhaustion. Shipwrecked, flogged, stoned, misunderstood, misquoted, unappreciated, he had run a hard race to that point. There were days when his body ached and his mind was weary and his spirit sagged to his sandals! But he counted it treason against the King to break stride. Paul was convinced that the Christian race deserves every ounce of strength in every moment of any Christian runner's brief hour on the racecourse. He stuck to that conviction. Weary, discouraged, sometimes rebellious, he did not relax his hard-driving spiritual stride. He was convinced that Christian victory eludes those who falter, faint, or quit. He was harsh with John Mark for quitting a missionary journey. He stated flatly that Demas, "having loved this present world," had forsaken him. He counseled the young church: "Be not weary in well-doing." Paul took Jesus at his word: "Whoever puts his hand to the plow."

The directive "keep at it" is wise counsel. The medical profession would lose stature if it were to announce, "We have overcome smallpox, diptheria, yellow fever, pneumonia, and polio. We shall forget cancer for a decade, rest on our oars, and savor our accomplishments." Thomas Edison's stubborn refusal to accept the kerosene lamp, coupled to his twenty-hour work days, contributed to his discovery of the incandescent lamp. Columbus, unwilling to believe the earth flat and willing to risk his life to prove it, contributed incalculably to the emergence of the modern world.

Constructive discontent with things as they are is a mainspring for personal growth and social progress. Whenever a man or a nation loses the desire to cross new frontiers, hard-won gains dwindle; growth and progress cease. The Christian race is won by individuals who strain daily after the prize of God's high calling in Christ Jesus.

II

"Forget those things which are behind." That is Paul's second directive for running well in the Christian race.

Paul was not suggesting that one should pretend that yesterday never happened. That is impossible, and it would be destructive if it were possible. The past is indeed prologue, but the present roots in it. Tradition as well as discovery, conservation as well as innovation, are essential to personal growth and social progress. The past did happen. Our roots, for good and ill, are in yesteryear. The past must be reckoned with. It also furnishes strength for today.

Some memories support, enrich, ennoble us: the remembrance of good parents, splendid brothers and sisters, confirmation vows taken in our youth, a teacher who loved truth, good friends, a beloved mate, a joyous child. So many memories enrich and sustain and challenge us. We do well to remember Lincoln and Wilson and Churchill, KajMunk and Bonhoeffer and Pope John XXIII. And we are always glad to remember Jesus Christ!

Memory, rightly used, is a precious gift from God. It brings an added dimension to human happiness and sparks social progress. Paul never forgot his own high moments in yesterday. He describes several in his letters: "I knew a man about fourteen years ago," and that dramatic day on the Damascus Road came back to hearten the hard-pressed Apostle. But Paul disciplined himself against living in the past; he faced each new day steadfastly. When he admonished others to forget yesterday, he was urging them to forget their past successes about which they boasted and their past failures over which they brooded.

To boast about yesterday's successes deadens the nerve of initiative. To glory in yesterday's achievements is to engage life at half efficiency today. No big league ball club wins today's game by telling the opposing team about yesterday's shut-out victory. No businessman achieves substantial success by boasting about his first "big deal." No surgeon operates skillfully today by telling his patient about the successful operation that was performed yesterday. And no Christian receives the high prize of fellowship with Christ on the strength of yesterday's service to him. Spiritual life deteriorates the moment it becomes static or adopts self-conscious airs over its comparative excellence.

Paul could have boasted about his Christian work. He could have gloried in his growth in Christian personhood. His labors were prodigious, and his person was titanic. He chose instead to search out and tackle fresh challenges day after day. When his life ended abruptly in Rome, he was making plans to preach the gospel in Gaul and in the Iberian Peninsula. Some of his richest writing was done during the closing months of his life. The gracious, practical letter to the Philippians is a "prison epistle."

Those who want to mature as persons, who seek to be constructive in the face of this world's desperate problems, will forget past successes, declining to boast about them. They will choose to remember that their significant successes owe more to God's grace than to their own abilities and labors.

On the other hand, man tends to brood over yesterday's failures. Past embarrassments, failures, and sins are hard to forget. Human nature has a perverse tendency to coddle the lapses of yesterday. Recall the story of the little boy who told his mother that his sore tooth hurt when he "scrunched down on it." When she explained that he should not irritate the tooth deliberately, the lad replied, "But it feels kinda good to scrunch on it." Something of that little fellow is in every man who broods over the misfortunes and misdeeds of yesterday. Human nature, undisciplined, wallows in past hurts, "doddles" over yesterday's mistakes, broods over the sins of yesteryear. It is easier to lament the poor judgments made at Potsdam than it is to work for an effective United Nations. It is easier to complain about an ill-advised marriage than to work at making something good of it.

Strong personalities will often try to repress the remembrance of past failures and sins. That too is destructive. Unconfessed sin festers. Paul, who had terrible things to forget, discovered that release from brooding over past misdeeds comes not from deliberate efforts to forget but through making an honest confession to God. He learned firsthand that God is eager and able to blot out sin as "far as the east is from the west."

Psychiatry makes a significant contribution to a fuller, freer life. But it cannot offer God's forgiveness. The penitent man, in the company of Christ, is enabled to pick up the broken pieces of his life and, forgetting the darkness and pain of yesterday, fashion something of beauty and goodness from the debris. Paul knew what Christ had done for and with the penitent bungler, Simon Peter. He also knew what Christ had done for and with

Saul of Tarsus—pride, legalism, "thorn in the flesh," and all! He wanted everyone to know.

The Apostle urges every Christian to forget past successes about which he tends to boast and past failures over which he is inclined to brood. No Christian can run well if he drags a wagonload of yesterday's little accomplishments and big sins behind him!

III

Finally, Paul reminds us that races are won by runners who concentrate on reaching the finish line first. "This one thing I do; I press on for the prize."

Singleness of purpose, intense concentration, exacting self-discipline are essential to success in any venture. "He had too many irons in the fire," explains simply why some people fail. Unfortunately, that can be said of many church members. And we do have "too many irons in the fire." We get so involved in business, so tied to a profession, so enmeshed in community affairs, so determined to maintain multiple social and cultural interests, so intent on (and contented with) our happy homes that we neglect our relationship with God except for an hour or two each week. Many who claim belief in God neglect as little as that. Only a few appear to have mastered the discipline of daily Bible study and daily prayer. Many faithful church members miss the joy of Christian living not because they treat Christ meanly, but because they have "too many irons in the fire."

Paul, whose disciplined life is a constant challenge, testified that singleness of purpose is essential to Christian living. Either one gives Christ first place or he does not. When a man seeks to make a go of his business, earn a Ph.D., be a competent plumber, win distinction in his profession—and throws his energies wholeheartedly into his work and has the aptitude for it —he achieves his goal. Anyone who single-mindedly seeks fellowship with Christ finds it. No one is ever disappointed.

Paul did not covet money, success, fame, or an easy life. He hungered after righteousness. He wanted to be like Christ. That was his goal. And he pursued it so steadfastly that he could declare, "To me to live is Christ." Augustine and Luther and Wesley were debtors to him. Christians in every generation have taken counsel with him to understand the faith that justifies and ushers in new life. He could tell that little Christian band at Philippi, "To me to live is Christ, and to die is gain" (1:21), because he really did not want anything inimical to the Person of Christ. For years Paul had been at loggerheads with God. Through Christ he learned to live comfortably in "the secret place of the most High." Singleness of purpose, intense concentration, and hard discipline brought him to dynamic contentment. "For I have learned, in whatever state I am, to be content." (Phil. 4:11.)

Paul's picture of the Christian runner prompts us to reassess our commitments. Each will ask himself, "What am I seeking? Do I really want what I'm getting?" Evidence piled on evidence supports the judgment that people in our affluent, technological, pleasure-seeking society are unhappy, neurotic, empty. Too many demand freedom without accepting social responsibility, pursue pleasure without purpose, look for an affable God who makes no demands. One cannot halt too long between two opinions without disabling himself. He must decide one way or the other. As this nation could not exist half-slave, half-free, neither can man live half-Christian, half-pagan. Paul has the decisive word: This one thing I do! I keep single-mindedly after the prize of the high calling of God in Christ Jesus.

The Apostle's formula for running well in life's race is disarmingly simple. Recognize that a good beginning does not guarantee victory. Pick up momentum by forgetting past successes about which you boast and past failures over which you brood. Keep an unbroken stride by seeking to know and do God's will.

That formula worked for Paul. It will work for you and me, because no man runs alone. Christ is at his side, encouraging, sustaining, empowering him. Paul could declare, "I have run a good race," because he could also claim, "To me to live is Christ."

6

Let the Redeemed of the Lord Say So!

The New England Yankee has a formidable rival in the Pennsylvania Dutchman at keeping his traditions and his money! In 1951 Trinity Church had declined to meet its modest benevolence apportionment, contributing only $5,800. An equally unrealistic current budget—$30,000—was expended for the upkeep of the large downtown church property, a dilapidated parish house, a boiler house, a massive parsonage, essential supplies, and remuneration of a staff of five full-time workers. The situation was critical.

As a conscious act of faith the clergy and the official board committed themselves to the position that Christian giving—like any Christian deed—roots in the *converted* heart and the *enlightened* mind. Holding to that position required that we take the long view. Biblical preaching, evangelical teaching, and pastoral conversations constituted our "program." Slowly, steadily, imperceptibly at first, the living Word in preaching and teaching and in hundreds of spontaneous and planned dialogues between the members and their clerical and lay leaders and with one another opened doors to the Holy Spirit. By 1965 the budget had increased ninefold. That year, 1,500 members gave $250,000 for the Lord's work in and through Trinity.

"Let the Redeemed of the Lord Say So," preached during the middle period of teaching stewardship, was designed to encourage those who were giving and to challenge those who were not. Dialogue, centered in the Word, continues to be creative. It goes on through spontaneous conversations among the members; a biblical-theological presentation on stewardship at each New Members' Class; panel discussions by laymen on the biblical character of giving; parish leaders who, constrained by the gospel, practice what they preach; and the deepening involvement of the congregation in the world.[1]

No single technique or method is indispensable to the teaching of

[1] Fisher, *From Tradition to Mission*, pp. 118-25.

stewardship. Any technique—pledging at the worship service, employment of the every member visitation, cottage meetings, team visitation, pledging by mail—which lets Christ confront persons through persons in that particular parish is authentic. Consequently, methods vary from parish to parish and across the years in the same parish. If stewardship roots in the converted heart and the enlightened mind, it requires the Holy Spirit who works mediately through the Word. It comes by waiting as well as working. Here, too, worship and witness are inseparable.

"Let the redeemed of the Lord say so,
  whom he has redeemed from trouble
and gathered in from the lands,
  from the east and from the west,
  from the north and from the south." (Ps. 107:2-3.)

Sermons, like institutions and nations, have histories. The first draft of this sermon was dictated on the evening of January 6 aboard the Manhattan Limited between Lancaster and Chicago. During the uninterrupted hours of that evening, I wrote a review of Paul Tournier's *The Meaning of Persons*,[2] read the gospel of John, and, before calling it a day, turned to an Agatha Christie mystery novel. At the very moment when Miss Christie's little Belgian detective, Hercule Poirot, began to unravel a mystery in his inimitable style, this stewardship sermon elected to be born. Hercule Poirot was abandoned to detect on his own, and the substance of this sermon was inscribed on a dictabelt before it could vanish into the night.

The critical study of Tournier's insightful book motivated the sermon. Hercule Poirot may have triggered it! Unquestion-

---

[2] (New York: Harper & Row, 1957). Parts I and III—"The Personage" and "The Person"—have been helpful to many parishioners.

ably, your persistent questions on the stewardship of money structured it.

Do I have the money to give?

Does this congregation deserve my economic support?

Is Christ interested in my money?

I

Do I have the money to give? Can I promise a weekly gift in view of mortgage payments, impending bills, the children's educational needs, the possibility of unexpected medical expenses? Have I the right to promise a generous gift in view of these realities? Certainly, family responsibilities come first. That is the gist of the argument which runs through American parish life. Unexamined, it makes sense.

At first glance it appears that some parishioners here, as in other parishes, should not pledge; their economic situation is precarious. Teenagers, retired pensioners, citizens on social security, and persons burdened by unusual hardships have limited economic resources. Human concern tempts this preacher to state flatly that this church expects no pledge from them.

But the gospel of God takes issue with this human concern. It presents a radically different point of view. The gospel calls every Christian to accept not only the promises of Christ but equally his demands and thereafter to confront all persons with *both* the promises and the demands. God, who evaluates man's response, expects everyone to give as he is able. Gratitude is not determined by one's economic situation, health, or worldly success. These factors affect the material expressions of one's gratitude; they should not determine it. Christian gratitude is at once spontaneous and disciplined. Job in adversity cried, "Though he slay me, yet will I trust him." God's thoughts and ways do collide head on with unconverted human sensibilities and ego-centered points of view. The collision is particularly painful for many when money is the issue. Significantly, Jesus spoke more often about man's attitude toward material goods than about his practice of prayer.

"Stewardship" is not a device for underwriting congregational budgets. It is not a spiritualized technique for meeting benevolence quotas. Biblically viewed, it is an act of Christian discipline motivated by gratitude to God. The Christian stewardship of money (and time and talent) testifies to one's existential relationship with Christ. Consequently, the church teaches stewardship to encourage its members to deepen their relationship with the Lord, to measure their deeds against the Christian creeds, to entrust their "treasures" *and* their persons to God, and to get the gospel into the world for the sake of Christ and man.

The Christian is called to the disciplined giving of his money. It is one strand in the costly giving of himself. Basically, the church teaches the stewardship of goods to encourage persons to rely on God who, in Christ, has proved himself trustworthy. "Why, even the hairs of your head are all numbered." (Luke 12:7.) "Look at the birds of the air: they neither sow nor reap nor gather into barns, and yet your heavenly Father feeds them." (Matt. 6:26.) A sparrow does not fall except the Father knows. "Consider the lilies of the field, how they grow; they neither toil nor spin." (Matt. 6:28.) "Are not two sparrows sold for a penny? And not one of them will fall to the ground without your Father's will." (Matt. 10:20.) "Fear not, therefore; you are of more value than many sparrows." (Matt. 10:31.) Conversion and growth in Christian personhood are integrally rooted in one's dependence on God. That is one reason why the church teaches stewardship.

This call to God-reliance, at odds with the American credo of "self-reliance," collides with common sense. It runs counter to sound judgment. It outrages one's sense of practicality. It is, nonetheless, an elemental strand in Jesus' teaching. Whoever dulls that teaching blunts the Word of the Lord. The point of Jesus' story about the widow's mite is shatteringly plain. The widow's lavish gift, made freely in spite of abject poverty, caught Jesus' eye as he stood outside the temple *observing* people's giving patterns. He praised the deed and commended the woman. Her deed and person judge anyone who jests about giving his "mite" to the church. They knock into a cocked hat one's pious notions that Christ is not interested in what one gives. Both the giver and the gift matter to him. He evaluates neither apart from the other.

Christ confronts every man in his freedom; each makes his own response. Here and there in vital congregations a few teenagers and pensioners, loving Christ, scorn common sense and tithe. Others, comfortably situated, outrun the tithe. Their sparkling generosity, demonstrating God's power in disciplined lives, prompts others to take a second look at themselves in the presence of Christ himself. There, some decide in their freedom to break with their material way of looking at life. Disciplined and spontaneous giving gladden the gallant heart of Jesus.

Those who save for the sake of saving and those who spend for the sake of spending are judged with equal severity by that exuberant, forgiven sinner who broke the costly alabaster box and anointed Jesus; by Zacchaeus who gave half his goods to the poor; by the widow who gave all she had. Old Lancastrians and "auslanders" must be motivated by the Word to examine their *careful* and *careless* ways of handling the material goods entrusted to them. We need desperately to learn God-reliance.

The question, "Do I have the money to give?" must be answered within the context of our historical situation. No

American parish presents pledge cards to people who are living under the heel of the Communists; it confronts individuals who are free to decide this issue without any political repercussions. No American parish presents pledge cards to people who cannot eke out the bare necessities of life, such as millions of people in India and China who go to bed hungry every night. Some American parishes *are* situated in economically depressed areas. The citizens there are our mutual concern, but "poverty" in the American vocabulary does not mean the same as "poverty" in the vocabulary of millions of Asiatics and Africans who starve to death in plain view of the world. In many places in America the Protestant parish reflects the affluent society. Certainly three quarters of Trinity's members have money to give! Selfishness and provincialism are the barriers we are breaching here. Converted hearts and enlightened minds are opening the gates to responsible stewardship in this parish. Christ is finding a larger hospitality in our midst. But there is still "much land to be possessed."

Responsible Christians do not ask, "Do I have the money to give?" They ask, "What does one give as a disciplined deed as he grows up in Christ?" Pledging and giving, inseparably linked with worship and witness, are deliberate and spontaneous responses to the gospel in the interests of personhood—one's own as well as others. Recall Jesus' plain spoken story of the man who built bigger barns to guarantee his personal security (the parable of the foolish farmer). That man lost not only his material holdings but his person: "Thou fool, this night thy soul shall be required of thee . . . [and thou art] not rich toward God" (Luke 12:20-21 KJV). That was God's unswerving judgment. Christian stewardship is concerned that things shall be used in the interests of persons and that persons will let Christ appeal to others through them. It is disciplined and spontaneous.

II

Does this congregation deserve my economic support? Is its proposed budget oriented to institutional aggrandizement or to the work of confronting persons with the Word of the Lord?

Whoever acknowledges *his* need for God's forgiveness, *his* dependence on Christ for the renewal of life, *his* hunger for righteousness, is convinced that every congregation—large or small, urban or rural—where God's Word is preached and taught deserves not only his dollars but also his talents and time and energies. Indeed, he accepts the gospel and shares it gladly. The people of God are constrained by the love of Christ to provide opportunities for themselves *and* for all people in all places to know Christ, to receive God's forgiveness, to nurture the new life. Consequently, they view budgets, pledging, and giving as means whereby Christ confronts the world.

Does this congregation deserve my economic support? Each must answer for himself. Here, hundreds of men and women and boys and girls come weekly under the judgment and grace of God's Word in preaching, teaching, sacraments, worship, counseling, encounter groups, and visitation. Is that worthwhile? Each must answer for himself. Here, several hundred laymen serve as teachers in the church schools and as evangelists in the community. Is that worthwhile? Each must answer for himself. Here, the official board and staff are committed to a 50-50 budget. Is that parochial aggrandizement? Each must judge that for himself. Here, a rising corps of members have enlarged the congregational budget fivefold during the past six years. Is that acceptable to God? Each will judge that for himself. Finally, God will determine whether we are profitable or unprofitable servants. To covet his "Well done" is to seek the only recognition which really matters.

The budget for this year, reflecting the official board's maturing concern for Christ's ministry, calls for a ten percent increase over last year's budget. Last year we overpledged a less demanding budget and then gave more than we pledged. This new budget would be doubled if the lagging one half of the congregation would join their maturing fellow members in disciplined Christian giving. Significant as that would be—especially in surging beyond the stated amount for benevolence—our primary concern is *not* the budget itself. We are concerned that so many members are avoiding proper Christian discipline and growth. Unconverted church members ask, "Does the church deserve my economic support?" Christians in witnessing congregations throughout the world ask, "How can I possibly be too generous with the church which shares Christ with me and through my support shares him with others?" Paul's description of the church in Macedonia fits some churchmen in this and other congregations: "They give beyond their means." Let the Holy Spirit hasten the day when that description fits Trinity Church from the newest confirmand to the oldest "pillar."

III

Does Christ need my money? Of course he does! We are not disembodied spirits. Institutional forms are one means through which the Resurrection Christ acts continuously among men. Christianity is far and away the most materialistic of the world religions. God's self-revelation has come to us through tribal myths, legends, stories, historical events, historical persons—Amos and Isaiah and Hosea and Jeremiah—and finally in the person of a little child at Bethlehem, an itinerant preacher-teacher from Nazareth, a dying man on Calvary, a Resurrection Christ with nail prints. In heaven's name, what could be more earthy than that? Jesus—bone of our bone, sinew of our sinew, flesh of our flesh—is God with hands and feet, finite

mind, and beating heart. He is datable—born in the days of
Caesar Augustus, crucified under Pontius Pilate, interred in
Joseph of Arimathea's tomb.

Christianity is concerned with the whole man in the whole
world. It makes no essential distinction (only functional) between the profane and the holy, the secular and the religious,
the laity and the clergy. Every person is called into the community of believers to offer his whole person in living service
to God and man. Christ's church exists for the sake of the whole
world; it is an extension of the Incarnation through us. Consequently, it needs not only our money, but our time, talents,
energies, prayers, worship, faith, trust, and obedience. Those
who overspiritualize Christianity distort it as gruesomely as those
who overinstitutionalize it. To accept Christ as Lord of all life is
every Christian's proper response to the living God, his reasonable service to God and man, his guarantee of authentic personhood.

Jesus, preparing for his triumphal entry into Jerusalem, sent
several disciples to obtain a donkey for his journey. He advised
them where the animals could be found. He told them that,
if the owner questioned them, they should say, "The Lord has
need of them" (Matt. 21:3). And to that sweeping claim that
nameless "owner" responded. *That* is stewardship: the practical
acknowledgment of Christ's Lordship.

Presently, however, the church, hard-pressed on all fronts, is
tempted to cajole, beg, and manipulate comfortably situated
members to give a few dollars for its magnificent mission. Too
often stewardship is viewed as a parish "activity," the concern
of a congregational committee, the special domain of an ecclesiastical "director." From the grassroots to the top eschelons of
the church there are sincere churchmen who rely on programs
rather than biblical preaching, theological conversations, and
personal confrontation under constraint of the Word. Until

persons are motivated by Christ to recognize that responsible stewardship rests on the converted heart and the enlightened mind, the church will tackle the needs of contemporary man with too little, and certainly too late, for many who stumble in the darkness.

The church's central need is to accept Christ as Lord. God's purposes are frustrated historically wherever his Son's authority is unrecognized, winked at, rejected. Obedience no less than trust is integral to the Christian faith. "Faith" which fails to persuade its professor to acknowledge and act on Christ's orders is sentimentalism, hypocrisy, stupidity, or a "witches' brew" of all three. The Christian, abhorring cheap grace, asks, "Do I acknowledge Christ as Lord of my life?" That's where stewardship begins and never ends.

The questions—"Do I have the money to give?" "Does the church deserve economic support?" "Does Christ need money?" —are presumptuous, patronizing, and, if persisted in, damning. Maturing Christians ask: "How much dare I keep without stunting my growth in Christian personhood?" "How can I resist giving beyond my means in the face of 'love so amazing'?" "Does my giving demonstrate that Christ is the Lord of my life?"

Now, let the redeemed of the Lord in this congregation say so! [3]

---

[3] For a decade the congregation has been pledging on a single Sunday during the worship services. Lay visitors call on the infirm each year. Periodically, lay leaders discuss the claims of the gospel (worship and witness) with the hundred or so marginal churchmen (annual communicants) on the roll of "confirmed members in good standing."

7

The Church with Banners Flying!

"The Church with Banners Flying," preached first at Trinity in 1954, aimed to cut the congregation's umbilical cord with "Old Trinity"—a gem of a colonial church (1761), the oldest church (1730) in the oldest inland city (Lancaster, 1730) in the United States; a "stately dowager," able to inspire nostalgia but uninvolved with persons outside or in the parish. The introduction to the sermon at its first preaching relied on one of *The Screwtape Letters* which still provides the title.[1] We fought it out on the thesis of this sermon.

Updated and employing a new introduction, the sermon was preached again at Trinity in 1964. This time the objective was to support and goad hundreds of parishioners who, in varying degrees, now endorse and act out the "thesis" of the sermon. Twelve years ago, it was a call to arms. In 1964 it was that for some but for most it was a call to step up the attack and claim new territory for Christ.

The first preaching of the sermon precipitated dialogue on the nature of the church which we have kept alive through the pulpit, the classroom, vestry meetings, counseling hours, encounter groups, and parish visitation. In the early years point one of the sermon centered on biblicism, cheap grace, the *formal* possession of the gospel, and the need for a confessional stance. Point two was amplified through discussions on the sermon and giving as acts of worship, the prophetic utility of the Word, and on witness through personal stewardship, evangelism, and service to God and man.

We continue to discuss on both points, but today the dialogue centers in the Inquirers' classes, the catechetical classes (13-14-year-olds), and church school seminars. It is also carried on by lay evangelists.

[1] C. S. Lewis (New York: The Macmillan Company, 1941), Letter II.

In its present form the sermon was also preached at a civic Lenten service in Cincinnati, Ohio, and at the Russell Sage Chapel, Cornell University.

On a crisp November afternoon in 1863 at Gettysburg, Pennsylvania, a tall, gaunt man rose to make a few remarks. The occasion was the dedication of the new national cemetery at Gettysburg. As the sun slipped across Seminary Ridge and poised itself to dip behind the Tuscarora Mountains, Mr. Lincoln, claiming less than three minutes, described the free society more persuasively than anyone has yet managed to do. In the course of his remarks he observed that "the world will little note nor long remember what we say here." The Emancipator, so often right, was wrong in that judgment! The world knows Gettysburg chiefly because of what Mr. Lincoln said there.

Today, a hundred years later, one can take Mr. Lincoln's words from their context and employ them to sum up the critics' judgment on the American parish: the world takes little notice of what is said and done there. One critic, Peter Berger, is jarringly blunt:

The most common delusion . . . is the conviction of ministers that what they preach on Sunday has a direct influence on what their listeners do on Monday. . . . The reality, of course, is that the person listening to the minister in the church is a radically different one from the person who makes economic decisions the next day. . . . In this second life of his the church is totally absent.[2]

Gibson Winter argues that the church has fled the central city to live in suburban captivity.[3] The Bishop of Woolwich, J. A. T.

[2] *The Noise of Solemn Assemblies,* p. 37.
[3] *The Suburban Captivity of the Churches* (Garden City: Doubleday & Company, 1961).

Robinson, argues appealingly in his little book *Honest to God,* that the church must effect a radical change in its formulation and presentation of Christian truth if it hopes to capture the world's attention.[4] Rudolph Bultmann, convinced that the New Testament is significant only for its underlying eternal message, calls for its demythologization, denying its historicity.[5] Dietrich Bonhoeffer at the time of his death appears to have been committed to a nonreligious, noninstitutional kind of Christianity— "a secular gospel." [6]

The twentieth-century church does invite criticism. The Russian Orthodox Church was an ally of the Czarist suppression of the peasants; the "October Revolution" fell upon it deservedly. The Protestant and Roman churches across Europe have been steadily losing touch with the people for two centuries and today have a limited influence in the life of Western Europe. In contrast, the church in America is a statistical giant in the ecclesiastical record books, but the effectiveness of its witness is by no means proportionate. The Word of the Lord is muted in many corners of the church by "success" conscious official boards, cautious pastors, and organization-minded ecclesiastics. No clear-cut conviction on the nature and purpose of the church has emerged from the parishes or theological centers.[7] In too many places the blind are leading the blind, the bland are counseling the bland, and "perplexed" clergy are following perplexed parishioners. That is one side of the picture. There is another.

First, church history records that however ineffectual or debased or corrupt the church becomes, it never sinks so low that it cannot produce a remnant. The body of Christ, however weak

[4] (Philadelphia: The Westminster Press, 1963), especially pp. 122-41.
[5] See *Kerygma and Myth* (Torchbook ed., New York: Harper & Row, 1961), especially "New Testament and Mythology."
[6] *Letters and Papers from Prison* (Paperback ed.; New York: The Macmillan Company, 1953).
[7] H. Richard Niebuhr, *The Purpose of the Church and Its Ministry,* pp. 17-18.

or maimed, is never a dead body. The Roman Catholic Church which fashioned feudalism did not die with the passing of feudalism. The Eastern Orthodox Church, once wedded to the Czarist state, appears to be healthier under the Communist regime than it has been in centuries. The Methodist revival in eighteenth-century England broke through the formalism of the Anglican establishment, gave a new thrust to Christ's ministry, and moved creatively into the world. "The strange thing about the Church is not that it grows old, but that it seems to have discovered the secret of being born again." [8]

Second, the current disposition to reject the church on the ground that it has not radically improved the social situation—especially in the last quarter century—must also be examined critically. Admittedly, the Roman, Protestant, and Orthodox churches invite censure for their uncritical allegiance to, or passive acceptance of, the social status quo in many places (the South, suburbia, South Africa) and for their cautious employment of the Word's prophetic utility in the face of political, economic, and social power structures. But these criticisms must be examined in the light of biblical evidence. The church exists primarily to save persons through the living Word in preaching and teaching and the sacraments. It is not called out and commissioned primarily to improve human conditions but to redeem persons. The church exists to save persons who, persuaded to worship the true God, are motivated and enabled by his Spirit according to their temperament and talent to fashion the good society for the sake of the kingdom of God. Many sociologists offer insights to parish leaders. They cannot, however, provide "chart and compass." These come from Christ.

Third, the church is not a human invention. If one accepts Jesus' word and the apostolic witness, he accepts the community

[8] Daniel T. Jenkins, *The Strangeness of the Church* (Garden City: Doubleday & Company, 1955), p. 14.

of faith as God's idea and handiwork. The church is the people of the new covenant, the heirs of God's promises to Abraham and his successors fulfilled in the person of Jesus Christ. Too many "church critics" in this generation either do not believe that or arrogantly ignore it. The church

is not an accidental, secondary element in the Christian faith—as if God had really willed to save individuals, who through misguided gregarious instinct and evil power-impulses mistakenly formed for themselves a community of worship. Rather . . . that the church . . . is a fundamental part of the divine purpose, willed by God and established by him just as much as the Incarnation itself. . . . The church, therefore, is a vital part of the gospel itself.[9]

I

The church goes forward with banners flying when it remembers that it is not only a social institution but also a unique fellowship—a redeemed fellowship—bought with a price, the precious blood of its Lord and Savior Jesus Christ. That has been the heartbeat of the holy catholic church from the days of Paul and Peter and Stephen to the present era of Dibelius and Niles and Pope Paul VI. Lacking that conviction, the church is a social-ecclesiastical institution held together by dogma, liturgy, and common cultural interests. To the degree that the institutional church lacks the conviction that it possesses Christ's victory it will falter under pagan pressure and attack, be domesticated, or take on the shape of the society in which it exists. The church is the Church wherever it accepts its unique giveness—bought, called, gathered, preserved in the Faith.

Martin Luther, oak of the Reformation, was an impulsive

[9] Langdon Gilkey, *How the Church Can Minister to the World Without Losing Itself* (New York: Harper & Row, 1964), pp. 60-61.

man. His angry alliance with the nobles against the dispossessed in the Peasants' War taxes his ablest apologists. His harsh attacks on the papacy reveal the "old Adam" in him. But Luther understood—as many present-day critics do not—the nature of the "new life" from which the "new community," the church, emerges. "I believe that Jesus Christ . . . has redeemed me, a lost and condemned creature . . . not with silver and gold, but with His holy and precious blood . . . in order that I might be His, live under Him in His kingdom, and serve him in everlasting righteousness, innocence, and blessedness. . . . This is most certainly true." [10]

This is the saving faith on which Christ builds his church. Wherever two or three gather, look upon the empty cross, and declare, "There was no other way; Christ died for me," and nurture their new life from the gospel and proclaim it, there *is* Christ's church. The gates of hell will batter this "new community"; they cannot overwhelm it. That is Christ's promise.

Admittedly, an uncritical reliance on a sacrificial Rescuer can calcify into rigid dogma; it can be fashioned as a verbal shibboleth; it can deteriorate into maudlin sentimentality; it can be dispensed as "cheap grace." But these caricatures of truth do not alter its reality. Wherever a few or many believe in, accept, confess, and act on Christ's hard-won victory over sin, the church comes into being, matures, and goes forward with banners flying. Christ's church is a redeemed fellowship.

Jesus was not a paid professional! "No man takes my life from me," he told his disciples. "I lay it down of my own accord." His voluntary act, therefore, is the crucial Event in human history. It is the foundation on which a "new community" of persons is built. It opens a "new age." But Christ's person and

[10] Luther's explanation of the second article of the Apostle's Creed, *The Small Catechism*. Joseph Stump, *An Explanation of Luther's Small Catechism* (2nd rev. ed.; Philadelphia: Fortress Press, 1960), p. 88.

deed must be accepted, appreciated, and acted on by individuals. Luther—believing and confessing that Christ had redeemed him, a lost and condemned creature, and acting on that conviction—made "justification by faith" the cornerstone of his dynamic theology. The early church and the Reformation church pulsated with new life and fashioned "new" forms to communicate that life, because it was convinced that Christ's sacrifice, claimed expectantly and acted on boldly, liberates man. When the church remembers that it is bought with a price, it is poised to go into battle. The attack is launched and sustained when it remembers equally that it was bought for a purpose.

II

The church goes forward with banners flying when it remembers that it was bought to do God's work, to carry on his Son's ministry in the world. The church is not a cistern; it is an onrushing river whose headwaters are in Christ. The church worships and witnesses to accomplish God's purpose.

Presently, some churchmen call for witness without regard for worship. Others insist on worship with little concern for witness. Both views are heretical. Worship and witness are inseparable. If worship does not constrain one to witness in the world, it is pretense: "Why do you call me 'Lord, Lord,' and not do what I tell you" (Luke 6:46). Christian worship motivates one to witness; it also empowers him in it. Evangelical witness is the continuing act of Christian worship.

Some contemporary critics of the church fail to appreciate it as a worshiping fellowship. Peter Berger writes: "Even those of us whose personal tastes do not run in the direction of organized religion and who feel no personal need for the sort of symbols that the churches have to offer can look upon all this with a great deal of tolerance." [11] That confession puts the critic into perspective!

In the hour of worship the drama of salvation is reenacted, the Event of God-in-Christ is focused on the screen of contemporary life, the holy God confronts man in his sin and, baring a Father's heart, bids him come home. Christ himself comes to worshiping man in the Word through the human activities of preaching and teaching and in the earthly materials of the sacraments. Some worshipers are indifferent. Others are moved to accept Christ as Lord and Savior. Those who acknowledge their need and accept God's redemptive act respond with confession, hymns of praise, and the giving of themselves to Christ. They go out to sin again and know it. But they also go out to witness—one to face a beguiling temptation with new insight; another to stand alone in some significant controversy because his conscience is captive to the Word; and still another to cope heroically with the newfound knowledge of a killing disease. The "new community" is at work in the world. Those who worship, witness.[12]

Man, searching out his real identity, will worship something or someone: sun or moon, wife or child, political leader or corporation, science or status, money or machines. That is his nature. Only fellowship with his Creator and life in the company of his Redeemer can satisfy man's search for identity, his hunger for meaning. That, I think, is what Tertullian meant when he argued that man is naturally Christian. Augustine sounded the same note: "Thou hast made us for thine own, O Lord, and we are restless till we find our rest in thee." Centuries earlier, the psalmist declared: "As the hart panteth after the water brooks, so panteth my soul after thee, O God" (42:1 KJV).

---

[11] *The Noise of Solemn Assemblies*, p. 111.
[12] See Fisher, *From Tradition to Mission,* section on Worship, pp. 129-32.

Until man turns from the worship of false gods to the worship of the true God, he will engage in dreadful monkeyshines, lose himself in blind alleys of meaninglessness, sink into dark despair. Every man needs to come under a judgment beyond his own or that of any man. He needs to be accepted as he is, understood, liberated from guilt, empowered to live, convinced that death is neither escape nor oblivion. Man needs enlightenment, hope, fulfillment. He needs Christ. The church offers him in worship.

Wherever two or three persons, or two or three thousand persons, gather to receive the Word in preaching, teaching, and sacraments, Christ is in their midst. This redeemed community, gathered to worship and learn, is motivated by the Holy Spirit to go into the world to witness. Actually, those who worship the God of the prophets, the Father of Christ, are more daring than others! "The worship of God," Whitehead observes, "is not a rule of safety." They are also more "worldly" than others. Wesley and his lay preachers got into the dirtiest corners of poverty-ridden London in the eighteenth century. Bishop Dibelius was denied his pulpit by the Nazis. Bonhoeffer was hanged for participating in the 1944 bomb plot against Hitler. The slaves, merchants, fishermen, Roman soldiers, and women who worshiped God in private homes and catacombs during the early centuries of Christian history got so involved in the world that the historian, Edward Gibbon, charged them (and the barbarians) with the fall of Rome!

When God speaks to man in worship, man is constrained to speak and act for God in the world. Jesus retired to Gethsemane; he returned to face Calvary. Wherever the church proclaims the demands and promises of Christ, those who truly worship are motivated to evangelize, to give beyond their means, to get involved with "civil rights," to demand public leaders who view nuclear weapons with awe, to be concerned about situational poverty. The people of God get into every corner of his world. The Christ whom they worship in an imposing cathedral, a gleaming new "church in the round," or an austere meetinghouse bids them follow him into the world and on to Calvary.

The style of witness varies from Christian to Christian. One is constrained to appear in Selma. Another takes a turn manning a Fair Housing Office. Another, holding membership in a private club which discriminates against persons, works to change the climate of mind there. And another accepts God's call to the full-time service of Christ. Christian witnesses differ in age, background, sex, talent, and cultural depth, but all are alike in this: they seek to bring their Christian insights to bear on the world Christ loved and died to save.

From time to time the Christian worshiper will recoil from this concrete witness, for the Word of the Lord *is* a burden before it is a joy. But, the love of Christ constraining him, he will finally venture, discovering for himself that the Lord's yoke is easy and his burden light. Far more worshipers witness in this world than anyone perceives immediately. Only in the perspective of history does one begin to see how Christians have held the world together. Finally, of course, the decisive judgment is handed down by Christ: "Well done," or "I never knew you."

The church—in hamlet, suburb, and center city, in the democracies and the totalitarian states—is under severe attack. It is often weak where it should be strong, silent when it should speak out, waiting where it should be working. Nonetheless, the church—ineffectual, debased, corrupt—never sinks so low that it cannot produce a remnant. That remnant becomes a mighty army with banners flying when it remembers that it is a redeemed fellowship, bought with a price, the precious blood of its Lord and Savior, Jesus Christ; and when it remembers equally that it is a worshiping and witnessing fellowship which accepts God's kingdom not only as a *gift* but as a *task.*

8

When Death Comes

Although the collisions with the middle-aged and older members at Trinity were occasionally fierce during the early years of parish renewal, these good people—who in those days "would rather fight than switch"—were met as persons. The renewal of Trinity Church did not require an angry exodus of longtime members. The dialogue between pastors and people rarely broke down. The critics were visited; their complaints were listened to and answered in the light of the Word. Further, their counsel was invited; it was heeded at some points, ignored at others. The critics, met as persons, were confronted with the demands and promises of Christ like anyone else in the congregation.

Although the older members requested this sermon on death, the widest dialogue which it opened was among the young families who had begun to appear at the worship services. It was they, not the older members, who pressed for another hearing of the sermon. Preached first in mid-July, 1955, it was, at their prompting, repeated that autumn. Mimeographed, it was carried into the community by many parishioners. It was preached again in 1957, 1960, and 1964 at the request of younger members in the church.

At Trinity we seek to approach all as persons through the preaching, teaching, counseling, and visitation. We aim to let the Word in judgment and grace confront everyone regardless of age, circumstance, or race. During the last decade, young, middle-aged, and older people have come equally (proportionately) to "Coffee and Conversation," Bible study, the book reviews, encounter groups, etc. Teen-agers in the confirmation classes (13-14 years old) are instructed on how to listen to a sermon. Ninety percent attend church regularly after confirmation. Encouraged to discuss the sermons with their parents and clergy, many do precisely that. Children as young as nine begin to take sermon notes.[1]

[1] See Appendix I.

Christ's church is not "a golden age club," a youth movement, a men's service club, a counseling center, a patriotic society, or a "civil rights" brigade. It is a redeemed community of persons, worshiping, witnessing, and serving in the world for Christ's sake. The church should be *evaluated* by sociologists. It should be *judged* on its fidelity to the living Word. The older members in the congregation first requested "When Death Comes." Today they are as inclined as the younger members to suggest and listen eagerly to a sermon on *The Deputy* (Hochhuth), the "new morality," *Honest to God*, "Handling Our Doubts," political extremism, etc. The notion that older people, Negroes, the culturally elite, "pillars of the church," youth, or the poor should receive preferential treatment fractures the biblical image of ministry.

"Jesus said to her, 'I am the resurrection and the life; he who believes in me, though he die, yet shall he live, and whoever lives and believes in me shall never die. Do you believe this?' " (John 11:25-26.)

Who, having heard it once, can forget Alan Seeger's poignant lament, "I have a rendezvous with death." Under the crushing weight of dehumanizing trench warfare in World War I, Seeger, a promising young American poet who had been called to the colors, focused humanity's attention on every man's wartime anxiety: "I have an appointment with death." Alan Seeger *was* killed, but war or no war, everyman must die one day.

Everyone knows that the human body ceases to function eventually. When death will come and under what circumstances it will come, God alone knows. Disease and accident and war bring a premature end to some bodies while others glide downhill gently but steadily across threescore years and ten. But in due time every human body is as lifeless as a dinosaur in a museum. Death, like birth, is common to humanity.

I

Whoever seeks to live a full life will face the fact of his own death. Everyone realizes that death is inevitable. Not everyone, however, comes to terms with the reality that *he* will die, that *his* loved ones will die, that *his* friends and neighbors and co-workers will slip from the scene one by one. Many Americans go to absurd lengths to assure themselves and one another that death is "not so bad." They camouflage it by the mortician's art, insisting that the funeral director create the illusion that death is a lovely interlude. Others avoid thinking through the implications of death by crowding their daily calendars with business, professional, family, and social activities. Nevertheless, busy schedules are disrupted as rudely by death as leisurely calendars are. Emily Dickinson understood that.

> Because I could not stop for Death—
> He kindly stopped for me—
> The Carriage held but just Ourselves—
> And Immortality.
>
> We slowly drove—he knew no haste
> And I had put away
> My labor and my leisure too,
> For His Civility—

Richard Baxter, seventeenth-century preacher, proclaimed the Word powerfully because he faced death biblically:

> I preached as never sure to preach again,
> And as a dying man to dying men.[2]

However artfully one may twist and turn there is no escape from death. It is the great leveler, the last enemy, the final event.

---

[2] "Love Breathing Thanks and Praise."

When a loved one dies he is lost to us and we are lost to him. The conversation and companionship and love we shared are gone except as one reviews them on the field of memory. The Christian service at the graveside is somber, downright jarring in its realism: "earth to earth, ashes to ashes, dust to dust." Everyman is "done in," literally, by death. It destroys the physical means which one employs to communicate, share, and fulfill his person. Unless God fashions a new medium for these essential acts of personhood—a resurrection body—each is finished by death, wiped out forever. Paul does not mince words: "The last enemy is death."

The ancient Greeks, notably Socrates and Plato, made an appealing case for the immortality of the soul. The Orientals comforted themselves with ancestor worship. The American Indian looked wistfully toward his "happy hunting ground." Philosophical and cultural discussions on these aspects of man's views on "life-after-death" can be fascinating, occasionally illuminating, in the classroom, over coffee, or at the local woman's club (especially at the meeting nearest Easter!). But those discussions are cold comfort when death invades one's family circle! In that dark hour one wants more than human conjecture. He wants assurance, a strong word from God!

Only Christ can speak that word, and does precisely that from firsthand experience. He died on Calvary. He also rose from the dead as he had promised. Consequently, he linked death *and* resurrection and fixed that link as an event in history. From the natural world where winter gives way to spring and flowers fade only to bloom again, one gets the impression that death begets life automatically, that resurrection "naturally" follows death. That is not true for man. Death and resurrection do not go together naturally for him. God's direct intervention was necessary to reverse the process. The risen Lord demonstrated that resurrection follows death for those who choose to do God's will. Simon Peter, who learned that lesson the hard way, was waspish in the presence of doubters: "We [do] not [follow] cunningly devised fables" (II Peter 1:16 KJV). Today, Peter might state his case in words like these: "We do not base our faith on a spiritual experience but on a historical event. We met the risen Lord. He walked and talked with us, and with others, too."

The suffering, death, and resurrection of Jesus are foundational to the Christian faith. Jesus' suffering and death, viewed apart from his resurrection, present him as a heroic character in a Greek tragedy. His resurrection, considered apart from his suffering and death, caricature him as a demigod. The former makes him a tragic figure; the latter makes him a superman. Both views are heretical. Either, accepted, aborts the power of God. Jesus—bone of our bone, sinew of our sinew, flesh of our flesh—ran the gamut of human experience. He was murdered that dark Friday at Golgotha; death closed in and conquered. His friends claimed a dead body for burial, using the tomb which Joseph of Arimathea placed at their disposal. Like any mortal, Jesus died. The book on his life was closed. The disciples were convinced that death had conquered him.

But God did not see it that way! As it began to dawn on the first day of the week, he raised Jesus from the dead. He clothed him with a resurrection body, even as he had provided him with a human body at Bethlehem. Both the Incarnation and the Resurrection are miracles. The biblical record testifies that Jesus' resurrection body was different from his earthly body (he appeared suddenly in a locked room). But personal identity was not blurred. He was recognized by his disciples and friends (appearances in the garden, on the road to Emmaus, in the upper room). The resurrection of Jesus was more than a "spiritual" experience for his disconsolate friends. They met the Master face to face. He walked and talked with them. He ate a fish dinner with two of them. He gave Peter and Thomas special attention because they had doubted the testimony of their friends. Believers in succeeding generations have been grateful to Thomas who insisted on poking at Jesus' wounds before he was convinced: "My Lord, and my God!"

The resurrection of Jesus demonstrates inside history that God is able to fashion a resurrection *body*. The Christian, convinced that he does not rest his case on cunningly devised fables, believes that his loved ones and he are not destined to be disembodied spirits, beyond personal recognition. He knows that death, still an enemy to be met, has been vanquished. Convinced that Christ, the pioneer of life, has explored the unknown realm beyond the grave and returned victoriously and that he shares that victory with the faithful, the Christian faces death expectantly. This realistic testimony by a young mother who lost a little child demonstrates the Christian victory over death.

Of course, I'm lonely for Marcia. You don't lose a child easily when you've had the constant care of it from babyhood. Marcia was such a tremendous part of my life with her tremendous spirit and vitality. You don't just toss it aside and say, "That's that!!"

. . . .

You know from childhood that someday you will lose your parents. It's a loss, but you have a certain mental preparation for it. You know, too, that husbands and wives sometimes die. You know, too, that many children are sickly and that sooner or later they will go. But Marcia was the Rock of Gibraltar, in perfect health, never sick. One day all was normal. The next day the whole world had toppled. "There is no cure," we were told. . . .

I've always read my Bible sporadically. I could tell you the stories. I could even interpret the meaning of the words. . . . Then one night after trying to be cheerful and telling Marcia to be patient, that God was her Father, too, just like daddy, and he wanted to help, I went outside. I walked several blocks on a houseless road. I thought, "I'm all prayed out." I felt like an emptied pitcher. All was gone and I had no more to give. And I remembered the motto I used to have on my wall, "Jesus Never Fails."

I thought, "He sure failed me this time. I can't go on any longer. I'm tired and worn out."

. . . .

I stopped in the road and looked up into the heavens and said, "God, I'm too tired to pray tonight. Just look after us." From somewhere came the words, "Come unto me all ye that are heavy laden and I will give you rest. . . . The peace which passeth all understanding. . . . Let not your heart be troubled." . . .

But how could I understand and get the comfort I needed? I said, "I'll read (the Bible). Just help me to understand what I read. I'll believe and understand. I'll take you at your word."

. . . .

Then one night, two nights before she died, I went out to pray. She had had such a difficult day. I ceased to pray for a miracle. I prayed, "I don't again ask for Marcia to get well. I don't ask for my cup to be removed. All I ask is the strength to drink that cup." . . . That night Marcia said her prayers, kissed me and closed her eyes to sleep. . . .

Of course, I miss Marcia and long for her. . . . The way seems long for me to go without her. But I never question "Why!" That is not important anymore. I know that I am at peace with the Lord, that he is real. . . . I am not queer or overcome because of my loss. I go about quite naturally and find more beauty in the world than ever before. I find that I want to talk about Jesus. I am no longer embarrassed to speak of Him. I want to. I'm so worried that others don't see that He is real, that without Him there is no life at all, merely an empty shell of existence. . . . [3]

The Christian faces death realistically and expectantly because he accepts the resurrection Christ and claims his victory.

[3] *The Lutheran*, XXXII, no. 16 (Jan. 18, 1950) pp. 27-29.

II

How does one approach a loved one or friend who is incurably ill? What does one say? We can agree, I think, that every person has the right to know his physical condition, especially if death is judged to be imminent. We can also agree that mature Christians are able to face reality. Accepting these premises, we still face a complex decision. Not everyone is Christian. Some people, including church members, cannot bear to know the truth about their physical situation. The decision is also complicated by the fact that "where there's life, there's hope." Christian realism is not fatalism.

If one concludes, after serious thought and earnest prayer, that no constructive purpose will be served by sharing a confirmed medical judgment with the patient, it is withheld. That decision, however, is made with fear and trembling. Whoever makes it—relative, doctor, clergyman—will be certain that his decision does not reflect *his* desire to escape involvement. Nonetheless, there are people who lack the inner resources to face death heroically. The unvarnished truth would turn their last days into a shambles. But who can and who cannot face death realistically is not readily discernible in many cases. That penitent thief on Calvary, by all odds, should have ranted like his partner in crime. He did not! The clear knowledge that he was dying had a constructive impact on *his* decision to turn humbly to Christ.

The decision to withhold truth can rob the patient of his deepest experience in life, meeting death with Christ, unafraid. Generally speaking, an incurably ill person should be advised honestly and compassionately of his situation. It is everyman's right to know if *his* death is judged to be imminent.

Then, too, there is another factor to be considered: "Where

there's life, there's hope." That is more than a platitude. Medical science is not an absolute science nor does it presume to be. There are cases on record where competent doctors erred in their diagnoses and where unexpected recoveries occurred. But these cases are exceptions in an era of medical competence. Each patient, therefore, should be encouraged to rely on medical science *and* to claim God's *full* resources. Meditating on the goodness of God in Christ, the ill person (like anyone else) learns patience with and confidence in God's ways. His relationship deepens and God's will is accomplished more fully through him. Paul prayed earnestly to be loosed from a physical infirmity. His thorn in the flesh was not removed; but God gave him the strength to handle his disability creatively. Petitionary prayer and quiet meditation open the patient (like anyone else) to God, giving him peace of mind, equipping him to face any historical outcome, convincing him that God resurrects. That was the experience of Marcia's mother. It should not be denied to any Christian.

It is the right of every human being to know the nature of his situation. If Jesus had asked God to spare him the knowledge of his own death, we could not look to him as the High Priest touched by all our infirmities. If Jesus had allowed himself to be deceived as he hung dying on the Cross, we would have been denied those precious words from Calvary. If Paul had been unrealistic about his impending death, the church would not have had his summing up: "I have run a good race, I have fought a good fight, I have kept the faith." Unless those who are responsible for the person of the patient are convinced positively that no constructive purpose will be served by telling him the truth, he will be informed honestly, forthrightly, compassionately. The maturing Christian, experienced in the faith, never loses sight of the fact that unexpected recoveries do occur, that more things are wrought by prayer than this world dreams, that God allows nothing of *permanent* harm or injury to engulf anyone who trusts in him.

III

Finally, it must be said plainly that some church members do not have a Christian attitude toward suffering or death. Too many are frightened, intimidated, overwhelmed by the prospect of death because they decline Christ's invitation to share in his suffering. They want the crown without the cross. They seek comfort above character. They hunger after success, not righteousness. They behave like permanent residents in this world rather than like pilgrims. Everyman must learn *and* accept that he is born dying and that no one is assured that he can pass from death into life unless he shares in Christ's suffering and death *now*.

The Christian is not sanguine about death. He looks on it as the last enemy, but in Christ's company he regards it as a conquered enemy. Consequently, he dies daily unto sin and lives in Christ. The Christian realizes that, although he continues to sin, he is a forgiven sinner. He accepts his new life as a gift. Disciplined, he nurtures that new life through worship and prayer, in Bible study, and through service to God and man. He does not welcome death. He does not view it casually. But he does see in it the release from the limitations of finite existence and the fulfillment of his person in Christ.

When one dies to his old self and lives for Christ—whether his new life begins at infant baptism, quietly in middle life, or cataclysmically in the closing moments of his historical existence—he knows that he has passed from death into life. He realizes that his physical body will cease to function one day; that it will disintegrate, return to the earth, be no more; that each fleeting moment of his existence is precious. He is also persuaded that the same God who provided his physical body for realizing and communicating his *person* in history will fashion a resurrection body for the full communication of his redeemed person. He accepts Christ's word on that, because he knows the resurrection Christ. When the gifted English preacher, F. B. Meyer, learned that he had only three days to live, he wrote these words to a friend: "Don't trouble to write; we'll meet in the morning."

Jesus said: "I am the resurrection and the life; he who believes in me, though he die, yet shall he live, and whoever lives and believes in me shall never die." He went on to ask, "Do you believe this?" (John 11:25-26). That defines the issue cleanly.

III

the gospel and the world

For God so loved the world.

—John (*John 3:16.*)

Go into all the world and preach the gospel to the whole creation.

—Jesus (*Mark 16:15.*)

9

The Human Contract That Matters Most

This simple sermon is placed first in Part III, "The Gospel and the World," because of the crucial nature of its message. Christian social ethics rest on the Christian character of marriage and family, for here persons meet each other in the greatest possible depth. Marriage can stimulate, strengthen, and encourage persons as the two partners meet one another with the judgment and grace of God, each speaking openly in love to the other. It can weaken and destroy persons when unacknowledged, unconfronted differences cause either partner or both to silence moral convictions. A couple's actual relationship with Christ will be mirrored most immediately and fully in the character of the home they establish. Christian social ethics, and commitment to them, begin with the necessity for Christian relationships in the home.

This sermon was preached in 1951 at College Church, Gettysburg, in response to the requests of college students, hundreds of whom worshiped there. Preached at Trinity Church in 1954, 1957, 1960, and 1963—the substance of the sermon is requested occasionally as a homily by couples being married in Trinity Church.

It should be noted here that "Mother's Day" in Trinity Church is observed as "Family Sunday." On that Sunday (and others, too) some aspect of marriage and family life is examined in the light of the gospel, the new sciences of personality, sociological reports, and thousands of pastoral counseling hours. The ensuing dialogue has mounted steadily across the years.

To some degree most sermons are autobiographical. "The Human Contract That Matters Most" is decidedly so. While the sermon reflects years of experience in premarital and marriage counseling, it roots existentially in my union with a gracious, decisive woman—a knowledgeable, maturing person. Perceptive and compassionate, she is an authentic person in the home, the parish, and the community.

Our commitment to one another and to our son has strengthened, enlarged, and brightened my ministry for two decades.

"What therefore God hath joined together, let no man put asunder."
(Matt. 19:6.)

A number of years ago the newspapers carried the story of a business syndicate's agreement to purchase the Empire State Building for $52,000,000, a contract which caught the public imagination. Early in 1901 a band of financiers and steelmen, J. Pierpont Morgan and Judge Elbert Henry Gary among them, formed the United States Steel Corporation, "the first billion dollar amalgamation." That contract jolted the public and stirred the social reformers to new activity. Shortly after World War II the United States government decided to give and lend approximately $11,000,000,000 to the free nations in Europe to foster their economic recovery, thus enabling them to be a buffer against the Communist bloc. That agreement, which made the Marshall Plan a reality, still staggers the human imagination.

Each contract caught the nation's eye because of its magnitude and dramatic import. But every day thousands of intimate contracts go unnoticed by any except the contracting parties, their families and friends. Yet the cumulative impact of these little contracts is more significant than the combined impact of the agreements which transferred the Empire State Building to new ownership, used the Carnegie steel works as the foundation for a giant corporation, and provided economic aid for European recovery. These "little contracts" which affect history profoundly are marriage contracts!

The marriage contract is a legal, often religious, always intimate, agreement which aims to bind a man and a woman in a life-long, exclusive relationship. It is the public agreement between a man and a woman in which each pledges to the other loyalty, purity, cooperation, service, and love. It is uniquely binding: each partner promises the other to have and to hold, for richer, for poorer, in sickness and health, *till death do us part*.

Certainly the disciplines and satisfactions of a really good marriage cannot be captured in print, but it is possible to identify its basic characteristics. The outline for this little sermon, therefore, is elemental.

Marriage is a serious union.

Marriage is a sacred union.

Marriage is an eternal union.

I

Marriage is a serious union. That should be obvious, but, unfortunately, it is not. Too many couples rush unthinkingly "to get married." A contract which commits two persons to multiple interpersonal relationships in depth for all of life should be examined seriously. No one enters lightly into a business partnership, and marriage is far more complex than any business partnership! Marriage involves economics to be sure, for two cannot live "as cheaply as one." But marriage involves much more than economics.

Marriage is intended to be a union between a man and a woman—a joining and blending of the physical, emotional, intellectual, and volitional elements of one *person* with those of another *person*. Literally, "union" means *oneness*. It is the acknowledged intention in marriage that the man and the woman will become *one* in body, *one* in mind, *one* in spirit. The marriage service requires that the contracting parties recognize and promise publicly that this new relationship will take precedence over all prior human relationships. Each is admonished to leave father and mother. Each is encouraged to cleave to the other. Each promises to forego any intimate relationship outside marriage. That rules out not only extramarital relationships but "innocent flirtations" and even the sharing of intimate family concerns with parents, in-laws, or friends. Marriage is an exclusive contract. It pledges two persons to an intimate relationship for life. It is conceived in honor and dedicated to permanence.

Marriage calls two persons to forge a real union. That is a bold venture. It is indeed a serious one, heightened by the couple's joint responsibility for children through procreation or adoption.

Physical attraction is a significant strand in the well-adjusted marriage—that certain smile, the touch of a hand, an eager embrace, the full act of sexual love. But physical attraction in itself is not adequate to guarantee a stable life-long union. Marriage involves more than sleeping well together, binding and satisfying as that is. Sexual attraction deepens across the years if it rests on broad mutuality of interests, on a shared concern for the life of the spirit, the shared desire for children, and on a wholesome *liking* for one another, an appreciation of one's own parents and the parents of one's mate, and the capacity of both partners to examine the strengths and weaknesses of each parental home, for marriage brings in-laws and ancestors into the new home. Physical attraction endures and deepens in those unions where the husband and wife share their maturing persons with one another.

Marriage is a serious union. It is not to be entered into lightly. But it appears that many people in our sensate culture give more attention to selecting a new car, building a house, or choosing a pedigreed horse than they do to choosing a mate! Where the initial choices are not made seriously, responsibly, and mutually, that marriage is headed for trouble. Meaningful marriage is built on personal qualities that wear well. That may not sound particularly romantic, but *real* romance is always a serious affair. Does he or she possess the qualities which in prosperity and adversity promise to make an authentic person? Marriage—intimate, exclusive, permanent, honorable, and responsible for the next generation—is not to be entered into lightly. It is a serious union "to be weighed with reverent minds by all who enter therein."

II

Marriage is a sacred union. The couple seeking to be united in marriage is vitally concerned with the union. Usually their parents and friends are deeply interested in the event, sometimes too interested! But God is interested, too. He ordained marriage. His counsel, guidance, and blessing are indispensable if the full potentialities inherent in marriage are to be realized. God is willing and eager to involve himself with the contracting parties. But they must call on him; they must acknowledge his demands and claim his promises.

Marriage is a socioeconomic union, a cultural union, a psychological union, a physical union. But it is more. It is a spiritual meeting and joining of two persons on life's most intimate plane. These mysterious interpersonal meetings, involvements, and adjustments—the collisions and joinings of heart, mind, and spirit—dignify and beautify the whole of marriage or cheapen and despoil it. These interpersonal meetings provide the existential context in which marriage fulfils persons, turns stale, or despoils human dignity. Any marriage in which persons cannot mature as persons is not ordained of God. It turns into a ghetto of the mind and spirit.

Because marriage is a spiritual union of persons it has theological implications. The rising tide of sociological, psychological, and physiological studies on marriage and family life have contributed much to our understanding of this intimate relationship. The pastoral counselor who digs into these studies gains insights which sharpen his competence for guiding persons toward and in marriage. But the exclusive reliance on one or several of these approaches provides a partial or distorted view. Marriage must be viewed sociologically, psychologically, physiologically, *and* theologically.

God ordained marriage; he created man and woman for each other. Christ, calling both to personhood, lifted marriage to the highest plane of interpersonal relationships. Because God expects the contracting parties to honor marriage, his church counsels each couple, admonishes them to view the relationship as a holy estate, and declines to marry them if they seek to enter into it lightly. God also makes the promise that, "although by reason of sin many a cross" may be laid on the marriage (accident, prolonged illness, economic failure, wayward children), he will not forsake those who enter into this relationship according to his purpose. But God's promise cannot be appropriated unless the partners accept his demands.

A couple may have a perfectly beautiful romance and a thrilling first year or two of marriage only to find their initially promising relationship slipping into boredom, ending abruptly in a divorce court, or sinking into sordidness, because God was given no place of honor in their home. Many marriages fail because there is no real religion in the romance. Each partner gives himself to the other, but neither gives himself to God. I am not suggesting that every marriage without God turns stale, goes on the rocks, sinks into sordidness, or ends in the divorce court. That is not true. Neither am I implying that the family who prays together *automatically* stays together. That is equally untrue. Marriage is too complex, its dynamics too vital, its nuances too subtle to guarantee it as neatly as that. Strong personalities, discovering mutuality, can love, marry, establish meaningful relationships, and fashion stable homes without so much as a conscious nod to God. Indeed, American society would be severely weakened if it lost these stable family units. But a significant dimension *is* missing in those marriages.

Some indication of the quality difference between a godless marriage of mutually attracted persons and a God-centered marriage of mutually attracted persons can be caught by comparing a Norman Rockwell sketch with a Rembrandt portrait; or measuring Irving Berlin's graceful little song, "God Bless America," against a Bach chorale; or pitting John O'Hara's *Ten North Frederick* against Herman Melville's *Moby Dick*. I enjoy Rockwell's illustrations, find pleasure in Berlin's tunes, and recognize some of my counselees in O'Hara's reports. But Rembrandt encourages me to pursue excellence; Bach moves me to worship God; Melville prods me to probe the depths of my being. The difference is dimensional and qualitative. Romance without real religion—marriage without God—lacks a dimension which is realizable in this life. There are Christian people, mutually mated, who have "Rembrandt, Bach, Melville" marriages! These unions not only stabilize society; they also enrich and transform it.

Am I giving the impression that Christian marriage is an idyllic affair, without struggle, free from hurt, pain, hardship? Certainly it is never that. Marriage is ordained by God, but it must be worked out on the earth by imperfect persons. Because the husband and wife are human beings, each brings grandeur and misery to the union. Because each brings to the marriage his own person and distinct set of life-experiences (mutuality in marriage does not imply standardization of being), there will be differences, discussions, arguments; there will be irritations, frustrations, hostilities. In some cases alienation will become so intense and prolonged that counseling help will be required. True love does not always run smoothly, but it can run steadily. Any husband or wife who says, "We've been married thirty years and never had an angry word," has a faulty memory or is married to a cabbagehead! Dr. Alexander Whyte once responded to a woman who made that absurd claim: "Your marriage, madam, must be very dull." Precisely. Very dull indeed!

When two decisive minds, two vigorous spirits, two independent persons come together in love and sanctify their union in holy marriage, there will be sparks and, on occasion, full scale "fireworks," especially in the early years of marriage. Across the decades there will be tense discussions about ideas, values, decisions, and persons. This will be especially true in the rearing of sons and daughters. Mutual judgment in marriage is won at the cost of personal growth in both partners. This "messy" human process of two minds learning to meet and function as a larger mind and two hearts learning to beat in unison is God's way of binding two spirits together forever. When the marriage partners tackle honest differences openly with a view to discovering truth, when they are motivated to help rather than hurt each other, and when they bring their differences *and* their persons under the judgment and grace of God—both partners mature as persons. That is the "messy," mysterious process whereby marriage becomes a union of persons. That is the existential character of Christian marriage.

Marriage is ordained by God, but it is worked out by imperfect human beings in unpredictable historical situations. Inside the security of marriage—sacred to its core—the partners work together and play together; they laugh and cry together; they hammer out their differences in worship and in work. Inside this engaging union of persons, ordained by God, both partners and their children understand and are understood, teach and learn, forgive and are forgiven, because they love and are loved inside God's encompassing fellowship of concern.

Before God's altar Christian couples pledge themselves "each for the other and both for God." Across the years as children become their privilege and responsibility that sacred promise is enlarged: "Each for the others and all for God." Marriage is a sacred union ordained by God.

III

Marriage is an eternal union. Every Christian knows, of course, that men and women are not given in marriage on "the other side of heaven's line." Jesus made that plain. Marriage does not exist "there" as we know it "here." The biological union, the political union, the social union, the economic union are dissolved. Gone forever are diapers, tuition, in-laws, mortgages, cocktail parties, and company vice-presidencies! Whole persons live creatively with one another in Christ's community. But the spiritual union—that holy association of persons as persons which begins here under God—becomes the perfected and continuing gift of God through eternity. Whatever there is of God's love (*agape*) in any couple's human love will enrich and steady their union now and, ultimately fulfilled, be meaningful beyond any knowledge of it here. Faith and hope will pass away; Christian love abides forever.

Robert Browning sensed a bit of this gracious truth because he accepted his loyal wife, Elizabeth Barrett, as God's generous gift in this life. Who can forget his persuasive plea in "Rabbi Ben Ezra":

> Grow old along with me!
> The best is yet to be.

The marriage vow is supreme among the promises people live by except for one's promise to follow Christ. It is the audacious pledge a man makes to his beloved and a woman makes to her beloved to have and to hold in purity and loyalty; to love and to honor in sickness and in health, in sorrow and in gladness so long as they both shall live. Aye, and in the company of Christ, through all eternity!

Love and marriage belong together. Wholesome romance and real religion are compatible. God ordained marriage for personal enjoyment and growth, social stability, and procreation. If a man and woman approach marriage with God, and work at marriage, and pray over it, and enjoy it day by day as

a serious union,

a sacred union,

an eternal union,

their marriage is ordained of God.

"What therefore God hath joined together, let no man put asunder."

10

God and the ꟼMan *Who Is* "*Different*"

For three centuries responsible citizens have aimed to enlarge the rights
of persons including racial minorities here in the United States. Honest churchmen have labored also to fashion a society in which all persons are treated as persons. Unfortunately, the breadth and depth of
these efforts have not yet brought a certain end to the crude and
subtle oppression of twenty million Negroes, as well as other ethnic
and national minorities in this land of freedom.

"God and the Man Who Is 'Different,' " preached in the autumn
of 1957, illustrates a "middle" point in Trinity's deepening involvement with people as persons. The opening paragraphs of the
sermon provide a description of its objective as well as of the changing mind of Trinity Church at that time.

In 1959 the congregation was "integrated" without serious incident.
The youth canteen, serving both races, received a Community Betterment Award in 1962. A corps of Trinity's members accepted places of
leadership in the civil rights movement. The staff, several vestrymen,
and a number of parishioners participated in three local demonstrations,
the senior pastor making the major address at one. Three hundred of
the thousand signatures on the Council of Churches' covenant on open
housing came from Trinity (1963). Several parishioners help staff the
Lancaster Fair Housing Office; three have served on the Mayor's
Committee; two played key roles in establishing and launching
a county-wide Human Relations Committee; and a half dozen serve
responsibly on its subcommittees (housing, education, employment,
etc.). The congregation also provides substantial economic support
annually for the community-sponsored Neighborhood Services, and,
in cooperation with several other congregations, enabled the local
Council of Churches to call a full-time Fellowship Worker (ordained
Negro clergyman) to serve persons in minority groups. The Worker

131

has offices in Trinity parish house. See *From Tradition to Mission*, pp. 133-63.

Trinity's widening involvement in the social and political life[1] of the community has cost the church a few members and a substantial number of prospective members. On the other hand, it has brought vigorous, outspoken people into its membership—decisive persons who abhor the insulated parish. They are powerful leaven. Steady gospel preaching from the pulpit *and* the pew fosters the mounting dialogue between Trinity Church and the community of Lancaster. To date the tensions have been creative.

In a nation which likes to think of itself as the land of the free, it is jarring to learn that the President of the United States had to apologize to a foreign diplomat because a restaurant in Dover, Delaware, refused to serve him. Mr. K. A. Gbedemah, Finance Minister of the Negro republic of Ghana, was refused service because his skin is black.

That incident, which occurred on Monday, October 7, 1957, was reported in newspapers throughout the world. America's moral prestige suffered another blow in Europe, Africa, and Asia. The debacle at Little Rock in 1957 was exploited freshly not only by the Communist press but also by the newspapers of friendly and neutral nations. The Hungarian "freedom fighters" were disappointed in us again. The West Germans were confused. The British barely masked their disdain. The French were positively caustic because we had been pressing them about their "little war" in Algeria. The Paris newspapers pointed out that France was using guns against armed adults in Algeria while the United States was employing armed paratroopers to force teenage children into school! The world does not view us as tolerantly as we view ourselves.

[1] See sermon 13, "Christian Context for Political Decision" and the introductory statement to it.

Morally, there has never been "time" for academic discussions on racial justice. Historically, whatever "time" we Americans have had has run out. Our overt and covert sins of prejudice and pride and sloth have found us out. Minority groups—the American Negro in particular—have had it. The seeds of revolution are sprouting. And the racial revolution, one act in the drama of democracy, will be played out on the world's stage before an audience that is critical of us, and in some quarters hostile toward us.

Several decades ago millions of people in all parts of the world looked hopefully to America. They believed that we were concerned about them. They considered us to be unselfish in our approach to international affairs. This vast reservoir of goodwill, however, has been depleted rapidly since World War II. We are victimized to a degree by the amoral propaganda of the Communists. But, by and large, we let our shining image lose its luster. We assumed that we could fight revolutionary ideas with platitudes, keep the peace with a contingent of Marines, and lately, win people's hearts with dollars. Our sins of commission and omission have found us out. Our moral and spiritual wells are running dry. America has been under God's judgment in every decade, and is now coming under the judgment of other nations, for its insensitive attitudes and selfish deeds toward persons (at home and abroad) who are "different" in color and culture.

For some time we in Trinity have addressed ourselves to this crucial social-theological issue. We have sought to bring the Word of God to bear on it in the vestry, church school, and parish organizations. We have counseled with hundreds of parishioners on the theological and practical aspects of the issue. Under the judgment and grace of God, the mind of this congregation is changing slowly. An open membership policy has been defined, a youth canteen which serves persons of all classes and races is in operation, a rising corps of lay evangelists is confronting the parish and getting into the community, a maturing sense of stewardship is enabling us to strike out on new frontiers. But the tempo of change is too slow among a people who profess to believe in Christ. We are not yet an integrated congregation. We have not matured to the point where our members look on all people as *our* friends in Christ.

But Trinity Church is stirring. The gospel is getting into the crevices of our hard hearts and firming up our soft heads. As one specific evidence among many, the vestry and staff have been supportive to, and are actively engaged in, fostering today's congregational study, "Christ, the Church, and Race," sponsored by our Lutheran Church Women. This sermon aims to challenge and to encourage Trinity Church in its rising concern for persons as *persons*.

I

First, let us think our way into the complex social-political situation fashioned by three hundred years of *de facto* segregation in America.

A restaurant in Dover, Delaware, declined to serve an African. We must face that incident openly and accept its inevitable repercussions. We must expect criticism and learn from it. Racial tensions have been mounting steadily since the 1930's. There will be many incidents like the one in Dover, Delaware. There will be hard skirmishes like the one in Little Rock, Arkansas. There may be pitched battles in metropolitan areas and in parts of the deep South. The Negro has had his fill of second-class citizenship. Revolutionary forces are on the march. The day is gone when Americans can fashion their social attitudes after the Coolidge dictum: "The business of America is business."

Examining the Little Rock debacle critically, we begin to appreciate the complex task which confronts not only the government but the church. The riots there on that tragic Monday were set off and fed by four hundred racists who beat up Negroes and newspapermen, attacked the police, ranted in the streets, and screamed obscenities at the white children who attended school. A handful of undisciplined people brought disgrace to a community peopled with thousands of responsible citizens. That undisciplined minority gave the Communists another propaganda weapon. They also rescued Governor Faubus from his role of false prophet. The church must rise and speak against this dangerously vocal, fanatically misguided minority in every American community.

That is one aspect of the complex situation. It also reveals that most churches must put their own house in order. Although 95 percent of the citizens in Little Rock abstained from violence, the majority did not actively support the integration process. They obeyed the letter of the law; they violated the spirit of it. Little Rock's citizenry, a majority of whom profess to be Christian, appear to have assumed little responsibility for bringing the undisciplined minority under the law. Those "good and respectable" people, like the "good and respectable" people everywhere, want order. But they declined to get involved in the "messy" business of establishing justice under law, the condition for order. That same lack of responsibility underlies our deep-seated social problems here in Lancaster. Those "good" German citizens who looked the other way when the Nazis took a Jewish neighbor forcibly from his home have many counterparts in the "good" people of this and every American community. Presently, the quality of concern among most white citizens—North and South—for persons "different" from them fails to match either the demands of the hour or the demands of God.

Social justice requires equal opportunities for all persons. The law of the land (unhampered by local laws) must guarantee these opportunities to all minorities. But a responsible citizenry must see to that. The church in turn must remind its members to be responsible citizens even though that will be interpreted as "getting into politics." Unless we fortify justice today we shall be called on to justify force tomorrow.[2] The church must also work to create a community mind which views *all* human beings as persons. A first step in that direction is biblical preaching which motivates and equips responsive members to accept responsibility for persons outside their own family and circle of friends. Biblical preaching irritates, offends, and alienates some persons. The church must learn to live with that!

A responsible society requires order, and order, in the context of freedom, rests on justice. Consequently, every responsible society seeks to fashion sound laws and to enforce them equitably. Dynamic faith in democratic principles and an active belief in God's Fatherhood will prompt the citizenry to enact good laws, to interpret them in the interests of persons, and to administer them fairly.

The church, North and South, stands under the judgment of God and history. It has not spoken responsibly nor acted courageously. The abrasive, debilitating act of segregation is accomplished every Sunday morning at 11 o'clock by millions of unconverted church members who sing, "There's a wideness in God's mercy." The most segregated school in any city is not the public school; it is the "Sunday school." No community will listen to the church on racial justice so long as the church declines to practice what it preaches. Beginning here in Trinity where the gospel has established a firm beachhead, we intend to let God's Spirit change our attitudes and practices. Then

---

[2] I am indebted to Blaise Pascal for this idea.

Trinity can speak with authority and integrity in and to the rest of the city.

Christ expects his declared followers to act out the implications of his gospel. All Christians pledged themselves publicly to conform their thoughts, words, and deeds to the demands of Christ, not to their own ego wants or to local mores. On race relations the gospel of God is plain: salvation is open to *all* people; God's grace is free; Christ offers his person to all in spite of the fact that none deserves his friendship. Christ, revealing the Fatherhood of God, calls persons to take their place in a family of persons beyond status, race, or culture. God wants a community of persons who demonstrate publicly that they are kinsmen. The foundation for that community is personal and corporate acceptance of Christ's Lordship.

Twentieth-century churchmen have much in common with the Pharisees of Jesus' day. Respectable, law-abiding, "religious," they act as though they are better than other people; they assume arrogantly that God favors them above others. Jesus' scathing denunciations did not fall on prodigals, prostitutes, Roman soldiers, or the dispossessed. His searing indictments were directed toward professional religionists, the socially unconcerned, the spiritually proud. He aimed to strip away pretense. He still does. Otherwise, the human heart cannot become a fit habitation for him.

"Religious" people cling stubbornly to the notion that their "religion" is for *their* group, *their* nation, *their* race. In Mobile, Alabama, the man who is "different" has a black skin; in San Francisco he has a yellow skin; in Denver he has a brown skin. So the game goes until, with razor-sharp subtlety, Protestant denominations can be identified by their orientation to particular white social groups! The Lutheran Church in America—allowing for exciting exceptions here and there—is not vigorously faithful to the gospel in seeking laborers and intellectuals, Jews and Negroes, Italians and Russians, Puerto Ricans and Indians. Our formal subscription to biblical and confessional theology has not broken our cultural affinity for North Europeans and their descendants—"our kind of people." With a mighty wrench which produced a splinter congregation Trinity Church decided early in the nineteenth century that God could speak English as well as German! Recently our congregation decided —with another hard wrench—to seek and serve persons beyond class and color. We finally admitted openly that ingrained provincialism and patronizing exclusiveness are not compatible with the gospel of God.

The problem which most parishes must face and resolve is primarily theological and spiritual: whether they can comprehend that God in Christ came to restore *all* willing persons to his family, and whether they will accept, demonstrate, and proclaim that saving reality. The American parish must orient to the Christian truth that—because natural man *does* prefer one person above another on the basis of color, culture, compatibility, and personal advantage (it's good for business)— Christ gave his life to create a new community in which persons are accepted as persons. Each parishioner must reexamine conversion and commitment for himself. The converted man, amazed that God has accepted *him,* rushes out to share the wonderful news that God accepts all persons. He also acts on this knowledge in making mundane decisions.

Many churchmen, however, are *not* converted. They do not want people who are "different" to join their churches. They shape their parishes in the likeness of their private clubs and island neighborhoods. They caricature God by casting him in their image—white, successful, literate, European. Wherever these views are challenged by gospel preaching, some members become irritated; others turn hostile; and in some situations, some withdraw from membership. This inner stirring and rising tension in the American parish should not be viewed as an evil to be shunned; it is a good to be embraced. Tension and conflict as well as peace and healing testify to Christian preaching and evangelical encounters in the parish and in the world. The gospel *motivates* persons to witness not only in the parish but also in business, politics, social affairs, and the family. Equally, the gospel *equips* them to witness if they discipline themselves to live under its demands.

Here at Trinity, gospel preaching and evangelical teaching have offended people. Some have declined to "join the church" and others have been counseled not to join. This modest effort to be faithful to the Word has caused discomfort; it has brought a measure of hardship. On the other hand, many parishioners are beginning to see that no Christian may trim the Word of the Lord to fit himself; that each must measure himself and his society against God's Word. Trinity's members are beginning to dialogue with and confront one another and their neighbors under constraint of the Word. New life is stirring in the parish. Every congregation is called to accept and live under the discipline of the gospel and to testify to Jesus Christ as Lord of the church and the world.

No one, of course, can *feel* affection for the three billion people in this world. But anyone *can* begin to do those things which he wants others to do unto him. He can admit to himself that if his skin were black, he would not tolerate the current discriminatory practices in employment, housing, and education which fracture "community" in Lancaster. At a deeper level one can let the love of Christ motivate him to treat other human beings as persons rather than as pawns.

Recently, I heard the story of a little child who asked his parents, "What are 'human beings'?" Patiently they told him that human beings are fathers, mothers, brothers, sisters, neighbors. "Everyone we know," the parents said, "is a human being." "But," persisted the child, "what about the people we do not know. Are they human beings, too?" The Cross answers that question with a resounding, "Yes!" If any member in this church does not like that answer, and if at last he will not accept that answer, he should withdraw from membership as a matter of personal integrity. Further, "church discipline" should reflect Christ's demands as well as his promises. Currently, the church decries "cheap grace" continuing all the while to dispense it! If, in fact, we do believe that no power except the gospel of God can overmatch the passions, prejudices, and fears rampant in this community and throughout the world, we shall demonstrate that belief. Faith without works is dead.

III

Finally, church members and clergy must wrestle with this question: "How far is the 'second mile'?"

The good Samaritan promised to pay whatever was necessary to restore a wounded man to health, cost be damned! Those who love Christ follow him into the world and on to Calvary. The "second mile" is not 5,280 feet; it is measured in terms of human need *and* the reach of the Cross. Christian discipleship *is* costly. Jesus said it would be.

No one denies that it is easier to sing about sacrifice in a well-appointed sanctuary than it is to take up a cross and follow Christ into the world. No one denies that cross-bearing is out of style in this era of noninvolvement. But the church must be firm; it must tell its members that Christ rejects those who reject him: "I never knew you; depart from me." The church must also bring the Word of the Lord to bear on the world's selfish values, provincial attitudes, and shortsighted programs.

The hope of the church lies with those (a minority to be sure) who, accepting Christ as Lord, are speaking the truth in love to persons no matter whose good opinion is lost, and who are sharing their earthly goods in the interests of God and man at some cost to themselves. These honest followers of Christ are admitting that they are not entitled to comfort and tranquility at the cost of hardship and frustration to their neighbors, and that they are called to be priests, witnesses, and counselors to their fellows. These are the light that penetrates darkness, the leaven that permeates society, the salt that preserves the new life. May the Lord add daily to their number.

We started this sermon with a closed restaurant in Dover, Delaware, a handful of screaming racists in respectable Little Rock, Arkansas, and decent persons here in Lancaster. The roads from all three lead to Calvary where we discover that no one is "different" in the sight of God. "All we like sheep have gone astray." (Isa. 53:6.)

Each church member decides for himself whether he will pay the price to follow Christ into the racial, cultural, and spiritual ghettoes of respectable communities. It is equally true that each member *did* promise publicly to follow his Lord.

11

God and the "Organization Man"

This was not the first sermon preached in Trinity on the "organization man." This one, however, focused exclusively on this acute per-
sonal-cultural problem. The sermon (1957), indebted to William
Whyte's study on *The Organization Man*[1] was aimed at local "corporate" life. Like other urban centers, Lancaster has the "organization
mind" not only in its business community but equally in its academic
community, hospital staffs, social agencies, labor unions, government,
churches, and public schools. Increasingly, it is difficult to identify
the individual and to locate the seat of personal responsibility in modern culture.

Americans—and now western Europeans—live with what Kenneth
Boulding calls the "organizational revolution." President Kennedy
discovered after the Bay of Pigs disaster how tight the organization
can be. John Le Carre's best-selling *The Spy Who Came In from the
Cold* provides, albeit fictionally, a devastating view on the organization's dehumanizing impact on espionage! The problem has not dimin-
ished in the last decade.

"God and the 'Organization Man' " was preached first in May, 1957.
Stirring heated dialogue in the parish and community, it was called to
a second preaching in November, 1957, and a third in 1962. It went
through a half dozen printings, the parishioners claiming and dis-
tributing 10,000 copies during a two-year period. This distribution
of the printed sermon called it to a secular hearing on forty-three occasions, 1957-1965, in and beyond Lancaster. There have been angry
letters, patronizing letters, and "provincial" letters. The majority of
letters and comments have been fair, concerned, supportive.

The sermon does *not* express disdain for efficient organization *nor*

---

[1] (New York: Simon and Schuster, 1956).

deny the necessity of institutional forms. Trinity Church relies on both. Quite simply, the argument is this: All organizational procedures and all institutional forms need to be scrutinized constantly to determine whether the forms are ends or means and whether the organizational structures are flexible enough to allow persons to be responsible and creative. Presently, the Protestant and Roman Catholic churches are wrestling with this crucial problem. The "organization mind" is *not* peculiar to business and management.

Too many "organization men" in business, government, education, social services, the military, and the church—insecure as persons or culturally naïve—cling stubbornly to institutional forms and organizational patterns which stifle man's creativity, blunt his sense of personal responsibility, and dehumanize society. Until automation antiquates the organization man or he is persuaded to a higher allegiance, the social-personal issue addressed in this sermon will be part of postmodern man's unresolved complex problems.

A germinal book, *The Organization Man,* by William Whyte, Jr., was published not too long ago. On the best seller list for some time, it will be read widely and studied carefully on into the future. It will be praised and damned. The book, competently researched and ably written, has become a permanent part of this era's literature of social criticism.

Mr. Whyte is not a carping critic nor an impractical idealist. He does not disdain organization. He does not advocate unbridled individualism. He is not a displaced person from the 1890's. He is a cultural realist. Mr. Whyte reports on a social climate which is inhospitable to creativity and inimical to the development of personal responsibility. I first read the book one night on a preaching assignment at Christ Episcopal Church, Cincinnati, Ohio. It was loaned to me by a young corporation executive there. I read it again as I labored over this sermon.

I

Who is the organization man? He is not simply "the company man." No honest mind denies that the organization man thrives in management. But he thrives equally in the labor unions, law firms, on foundation and hospital staffs and university faculties, in welfare organizations, public school systems, all branches of local, state, and federal government, and in the institutional church (parishes as well as boards and agencies). He works for the organization. He takes his vows to the organization. Bit by bit he blunts his innate creativity and weakens his God-given capacity for responsible personhood by first accepting and then yearning after the multiple benefits which the organization distributes to its loyal supporters. It is not putting it too strongly to suggest that the organization man gives his soul in exchange for group acceptance and material security. Unaware of or ignoring Jesus' uncompromising judgment that one must seek first the kingdom of God or lose his person, the organization man neglects the opportunities for self-realization. He exerts little effort to reverse the current trend to exalt group behavior. He accepts the notion that group "creativity" is superior to individual creativity. Consequently, a new socio-economic-political pattern is emerging which calls for teams of executives to run industry, committees to fashion education, commissions to define the mind of church and state. This new cultural view submerges the individual in the group, confuses "togetherness" with "community," and breeds conformity. Inevitably, it fosters intellectual and spiritual mediocrity and loses man in the masses.

The good team player, the easy cooperator, the uncritical "good Joe"—no matter how few ideas he provides—is preferred in too many places to the "prickly," critical, creative thinker. The valued man is the one who fits easily into the group, able to reconcile diverse points of view without concerning himself about the rightness of one view or another. Harmony, efficiency, and production are the goals to be achieved. Change, fluidity, and conflict are evils to be shunned. Independent thinkers must be brainwashed, shelved, or screened from the organization; the highest art is administration. But efficient administration—needful in a technological society—stifles creativity wherever it becomes an end in itself. If creative persons are lost in committees, teams, and commissions, there will be a dearth of creative ideas. Efficient administration will exist without any purpose. The results of this are plainly evident in contemporary culture: conformity, civilized affability, mediocrity, false security, a pseudoclassless society, a pious patriotism. The "organization people" do not fight Christian community; they simply do not understand it. Collectivization is fostered in the name of community.

Responsible social critics do not call for a return to "rugged individualism." They do not prefer the "robber baron" to the "organization man!" They do not suggest a return to the fragmentary life which plagued Western man during the late Middle Ages. They do recognize, however, that "belongingness" in terms of secular goals—mechanically and situationally fostered —is not less destructive to man's *creative* processes than the old patterns imposed by rugged individualism.

The group exists to execute ideas; it does not produce them. The administrator does not understand the conditions of creativity: the messiness of intuition, the aimless thoughts, the impractical questions. These realities, which are companions to discovery, are anathema in the world of the administrator. Order, harmony, consensus, and production are his proper goals.[2]

[2] *Ibid.*, p. 224.

Jefferson and Adams, unhindered by an "administrator," provided both the substance and the form of the Declaration of Independence. The American labor movement took shape, albeit messily, when creative leaders came forward—Samuel Gompers, Eugene V. Debs, and Illinois' intrepid governor (1903), John Altgeld. Louis Pasteur did not rely on a conference of his medical peers to advance science. Beethoven did not chair a committee to compose the *Ninth Symphony*. Luther did not check a "Gallop Poll" before he made his ringing declaration at the Diet of Worms. Individual creativity and personal responsibility are indispensable to a dynamic community of persons.

The current climate of organization thinking, fostered and undergirded by group doctrine, makes creative personalities suspect. The cooperative employee wins advancement; the independent thinker is isolated. Increasingly, the key man is the expediter, the manager, the compromiser. The subsequent flight from excellence and a conformity which smothers personhood are exorbitant prices to pay for material productivity and affluence.

Consider the institutional church. The Reformation church, like its apostolic progenitor, took strength initially from its conviction that ultimate authority resides in God's Word; that this authority is communicated through his Word in preaching, teaching, and sacraments; that authentic community is fashioned by individual Christians who, prompted and sustained by the Holy Spirit, exercise Christ's ministry; and that this "new community" exists for worship and witness, nurture and mission. But the reformers, like the apostles, accepted reality: a spirit-filled ministry requires institutional forms.

From the beginning the Christian church fashioned evangelical forms to embrace and care for *persons* in the community, to preserve apostolic truth, and to carry the gospel into the world. Christianity has been able to bridge the centuries by providing a Spirit-inhabited institution through which the Word could become flesh in every generation. Led by the Holy Spirit, the church shapes historical forms through which Christ can confront persons in time, forms within which it can *be* and through which it can accomplish God's mission. The sixteenth-century Reformation was, in part, a criticism of the institutionalized Christianity developed during the Middle Ages, but the reformers did not reject institutional forms for carrying on a Spirit-filled ministry. Organization is needful.

But when the church gets preoccupied with organization and liturgy and dogma as ends rather than means; when it seeks, however graciously, to pressure individual congregations to adopt uniform stewardship programs; and when it fails to encourage vital theological conversations (as though the organization church were the depository of all truth), institutionalism is hurtful rather than helpful. Efficient organization and relevant institutional forms can provide channels for the creative work of the Holy Spirit, but the machinery and the forms must be examined constantly to determine whether they are helpful or hurtful in confronting persons with the Word of the Lord.

Obviously, one must fight the organization mind in the local congregation. Many parishioners want to trim God's truth so that it offends no one. They seek subtly and boldly to reduce Christianity to the level of one religion among many, to compromise the faith so that the world inside the church is comfortable with it, to use Christ's message to exploit belief as a technique for achieving earthly goals and escaping tensions inherent in responsible living. The real threat to dynamic Christian leadership does not come from the handful of neurotics in every parish who, if kindly but firmly withstood, will either isolate themselves from the main body of members or finally be persuaded to accept the way which they initially resisted. It comes from the affable majority who prefer the programmatic approach to the prophetic stance. The Word of the Lord, which comes with fire and healing, collides inevitably with spiritual mediocrity and anti-intellectualism in the parish and with ecclesiasticism in the church-at-large.

II

Where does the organization man breed? Who conceived him? Who nursed him to maturity?

The organization man was conceived and nursed to resilient strength in a majority of American homes where emotional security was lacking and communal relationships did not encourage children to think for themselves, act on their judgments, and accept the consequences of their decisions. He got plenty of good food, adequate clothing, and twelve years in school. One in every three received a college education. But his home and school were not equal to fashioning him for responsible personhood. He was reminded to look out for "number one" (no one else will), advised not to stick his neck out (don't volunteer), counseled to "go along to get along." Home, school, and church combined to foster selfishness, noninvolvement, and conformity.

The "organization child" is distinguishable before he enters first grade. In many schools the deadening process continues. Individuality and creativity are minimized in the name of democratic education, as though it were possible to level men's unequal and diverse gifts. The students get the impression that group relationships are more important than intellectual disciplines. In reality these constitute one essential for authentic personal and interpersonal relationships.

The situation is not notably different in the "silent generation," the "conforming generation," the "careful generation." Their acknowledged goal is security within the group. Generally, the curricula of colleges and universities are directed toward

developing vocational competence rather than critical-minded-
ness, social consciousness, personal involvement. The graduates
are equipped for business and professional specialties. Critical,
creative, daring thinking is not fostered widely. Most graduates
are shaped for organization life.[3]

There is a strong disposition among many Americans to have
some group or organization tell them what to do and how to
do it. They are eager for group approval and economic security.
Two decades ago the Harvard Report concluded that "too
many have learned too little about too much."[4] That climate
is hospitable to the organization mind. The organization, demanding conformity, fosters the mediocrity which Henry
Wallace in the late 1940's sought to glorify as "the common
man." The truth that God fashioned an *uncommon* man and
in Christ endured humiliation, pain, and death because *he*
views his creation as being potentially like him is a truth which
has little impact on contemporary American culture.

Before we examine a better way of life for the organization
man, let me point to several particularly significant chapters in
Mr. Whyte's book: "The Fight against Genius," "The Bureauc-
ratization of the Scientist," "The Church of Suburbia," "The
Organization Children," and "Love That System." The chapter, "Love That System," points up the rising victory of the
social ethic over the personal ethic. Mr. Whyte brings this threat
into sharp focus by identifying some striking reflections of it in
modern literature. Examining Herman Wouk's *The Caine
Mutiny,* he points out how the novel depicts the changing pat-

---

[3] What was said in the 1957 sermon has not been deleted. There is no firm evidence that the youth who crusade in the South, criticize government policies in
Vietnam, and riot here and there (Berkeley) are a majority. There have been stir-
rings, but most young people continue to "play it cool." Too many youth still seek
security and group acceptance.

[4] *Report on General Education in a Free Society* (Cambridge: Harvard University
Press, 1945), p. 147.

terns of personal responsibility in our day. He points similarly to Sloan Wilson's *The Man in the Gray Flannel Suit*. Both novelists describe contemporary man's flight from personal responsibility.

There are no substitutes for initiative, ability, courage, decisiveness, and a sense of personal responsibility. But these qualities do breed conflict between persons. Our frantic efforts to eliminate conflict and our pathetic dodges to escape personal suffering lead us to undervalue, and in some quarters to disdain, these essential qualities. The motion picture *High Noon*—a bit of screen artistry—won the New York Drama Critics Award in 1952. The award-winning movie reflects the old Protestant ethic —the sense of personal responsibility. The sheriff accepted *his* responsibility to stand against a bloc of criminals even though the townspeople ran for cover and his bride-to-be begged him to leave town. There simply is no substitute for personal responsibility.

III

Is there a better way of life for the organization man? What does Mr. Whyte suggest?

Recognizing that one cannot turn back the clock, the author accepts the organization as the necessary means for executing ideas and achieving production. He argues for enlightened, responsible individualism and a more flexible organization in which individuals can exercise their creativity. Mr. Whyte pleads for each to stand up in the name of creativity and "fight The Organization." [5] His analysis of a complex social problem is perceptive, stimulating, helpful. But his plea, from the Christian point of view, is unrealistic! Who is able to fight the organization—indefatigably?

[5] *The Organization Man*, p. 404.

First, some people have a temperament which constrains them to rebel simply for the sake of rebellion. They bounce from job to job, managing little more than high-flung speeches about *their* rebellion. At best, this minority focuses attention on the problem, but these "rebels" do not offer constructive answers to it. Their resistance to the organization is ineffectual.

Second, some intellectuals, firmly grounded in the sciences and the humanities, are able to withstand the rigors of deadly organization. Enriched by liberal arts training—able to appreciate science, technology, art, literature, history, and organization—this minority (C. P. Snow and S. E. Morison, for example) are able to work in and through the organization without losing their identity as persons. They are not able, however, to *transform* it. They modify trends, blunt harsh emphases, and refine goals. They maintain their integrity as persons in the process. But the intellectual aristocrats lack the spiritual resources, the emotional resilience, and the numerical strength to refashion the organization mind.

Third, there is an occasional individual who stands head and shoulders above the rebel and the intellectual aristocrat. He is that rare genius who, like Augustine, Luther, Lincoln, and Churchill, finds a great cause and single-mindedly allies his multiple-talented person with it. He not only stands against the organization; he also exerts a salutary impact on it, sometimes altering it during his moment of leadership. But his impact is not enough to transform it.

If the rebel, the intellectual aristocrat, and the genius cannot transform the organization mind, and if Mr. Whyte's plea to "fight the Organization" is unrealistic, what hope is there? Has the cult of conformity conquered? Is modern man doomed to be an "outer-directed" person? Is George Orwell's *Nineteen Eighty-Four* inevitable?

Whoever accepts Christ as his Lord is motivated and enabled

to mature as a person inside the organization while he works in, for, and through it. He is also equipped from the gospel to transform his segment of the organization. Any person who gives himself to the truth—not in philosophical abstraction or in organizational part, but as it is revealed in the person of Christ— is empowered to live creatively in *any* society. Whoever commits himself to Christ is enabled to stand against the organization charitably, constructively, sacrificially. Christ's man not only keeps his integrity; he also shares it with the organization. He is leaven, light, salt. This twice-born person actually refashions his corner of the organization.

Mr. Whyte pleads with contemporary man to fight the organization. His plea is well intentioned. But every man has a breaking point, a moment when he gives ground, flees excellence, and conforms unless he is judged, enlightened, renewed, and sustained by a Person who never gives up or gives in; who stands creatively in every situation; who fashions new forms because he has a new spirit to fill them—a Person whose identification with God is so complete as to be an Incarnation—the Lord Christ. Men of high and low estate, committing themselves to Christ, have been enabled from the first Christian century to the present troubled era to stand for truth against any system and to resist any organization which attacks or subverts truth.

It is the unique character of the Christian religion to reveal truth as objective reality in the historical person of Jesus and thereafter to point to the resurrection Christ as the one who motivates and equips persons to be faithful to truth. Consequently, Christ's men not only stand up to collectivism in state, school, and church, business and industry, union and management, leisure and recreation; they also transform any society through their participation in it. Salvation is not only eschatalogical; it is mundane.

Let every church member be persuaded that the answer to

the Organization Man is the Man of God. This new creature walks in the land of the organization, understands and speaks the language of the organization yet thinks, speaks, acts, and lives with insights and values which root in and stem from his relationship with God.

So the church of Christ pleads Sunday after Sunday and every day of the week for men and women and boys and girls to take their place in this spiritual aristocracy which acknowledges Christ as Lord of Lords and King of Kings. Christ transforms organization into community because he refashions manipulators and cowards, big operators and crooks, cautious little people and parasites, into authentic persons. Christ's man is God's answer to the organization man.

12

Can Christianity Overmatch Communism?

Christian commitment and concerned citizenship prompted and have sustained my continuing interest in Marxist doctrine. Training as a historian sharpened this study of Communist doctrine as it adapts to and concretes itself in national states. Consequently, this sermon (substance) was first preached in 1946. In those distant days some parishioners "felt" that the preacher did not appreciate America's wartime ally, Russia. When the sermon was preached at intervals, 1948-1962, new critics came forward to charge that the preacher was "soft on communism!" The sermon's basic thrust, framed in 1946, expanded in 1948, set in its present form in 1954, and sharpened in 1962, has remained substantially unaltered. The structure comes from a conversation with Elton Trueblood at Lake Chatauqua in 1951. The printed sermon employs an updated introductory paragraph.

When the gospel constrained Trinity's pulpit to confront McCarthyism in 1954 (the Senator was the featured speaker for the annual meeting of the Lancaster Manufacturers' Association), a trilogy of sermons was announced: 1) the one included here; 2) a documented critique on "McCarthyism" in the light of the gospel; and 3) "Christianity's Call to Voluntary Revolution." What happened as a result of the "McCarthy sermon" (fat, affluent, uncritical 1954 was an uneasy year for prophets) is recounted in *From Tradition to Mission*, pp. 60-63. A vestryman forwarded the trilogy to the Freedoms' Foundation Committee; a George Washington Medal was awarded in 1954 for the sermon (substance) included here.

During the early 1960's when extremists were winning a fresh following in Lancaster County, concerned parishioners asked for a critical evaluation of the strident voices on the "far right" and for another appraisal of communism ("far left"). This sermon was preached back-to-back with one titled, "God and the Super-Patriots."

Mimeographed copies of both sermons were distributed by the parishioners. *The Lutheran* carried, "Can Christianity Overmatch Communism?" "God and the Super-Patriots" gained a wide hearing in the community.

Communism has been, is, and continues to be a powerful revolutionary force in the world. The church should help its members understand this historical movement; equip them to criticize competently its false views of man, society, and God; and empower them to meet it constructively. That it is not a dead issue in world politics and diplomacy is currently (1966) demonstrated by the sharp controversy over Vietnam. Communist China and the emerging national states in Africa present a formidable challenge to world peace and international security. An informed church can contribute to an imaginative, bold addressment of these international issues. Responsible preaching on political and social issues and serious study groups in the parishes are indispensable to the church's effective witness. As one example, the forum use of the materials on "Great Decisions" (Foreign Policy Association) has enlarged Trinity's mind on some complex contemporary issues.

Our citizenry is acquainted with the "cold war" and the several score of hot wars in this revolutionary postwar era. They know about "containment policy," NATO, SEATO, and the United Nations. Over luncheon counters, in taverns, at ball games, during business conferences, and at cocktail parties they talk about communism, the rise of Red China, nuclear weapons, retaliatory force, unilateral action, and Huxley's "brave new world." They present opinions and argue points of view on the Korean War, the French withdrawal from Vietnam and Algeria, the merits of Dag Hammarskjöld, the competence of Dean Rusk, and the "free way of life." Too often, however, these exchanges and discussions produce more heat than light. A free society requires an enlightened citizenry.

One glaring lack in many citizens' discussions is the spotty knowledge which these people exhibit about historical communism, its philosophical premises, and its variations in sovereign states. When churchmen talk about the crucial struggle between Christianity and communism for the hearts and minds of men, it is evident—especially in lay circles—that few understand the basic differences between the two. Christianity is a way of life with God through faith in Jesus Christ which liberates and dignifies man who seeks to fashion a state which serves persons. Communism is commitment to a material way of looking at life and rigid adherence to tenets which deny the value of persons over and against the interests of an authoritarian state. Until many *citizens* in the free world—and Christians ought to lead the way—can dissect Communist philosophy competently, expose its amoral program effectively, and creatively overmatch its passion, the free *nations* are not likely to cope with this centuries-old world view.

Unfortunately, some "anti-Communists," especially in America, are unduly impressed by the rise and spread of communism. Preoccupied with its successes but silent on its massive failures, unresolved tensions, and inner conflicts, these avowed enemies of communism forge a psychology of defeat by implying that its victory is inevitable. Their "scare tactics" alternately confuse, discourage, and paralyze elements of our citizenry. They also embarrass, irritate, and occasionally alienate "ally" and "neutral" nations. Consequently, enlightened citizens abhor those tactics. But in combating them, they occasionally give the impression that they consider communism to be no threat at all.

Critical Christian minds are alert to both errors. They are not sanguine about Communists, radical rightists, or citizens who rest secure on military power. Further, they recognize that the Christian community is not only a minority today but also a diminishing minority because of the world's population explosion; the fresh missionary thrusts of "competing" world religions; the ineptitude of their own missionary strategy at home and abroad; the secularization of Western man; and communism's clever and ruthless efforts to domesticate, and in some places to liquidate, the church. Neither Christianity nor democracy is having an easy time of it these days.

Nonetheless, knowledgeable people do not panic. They are not thrown off balance by Soviet Russia's shifting stances nor intimidated by the emergence of Red China as a nuclear power. They recognize that the situation is precarious but not hopeless. The outcome of *any* human situation is problematical until it is actually determined. Washington and his valiant compatriots could have quit at Valley Forge. Napoleon's defeat at Waterloo was not foreordained. The United Nations is not destined to fail. History is written by men, not IBM machines. Human convictions, judgments, and courage are decisive factors in any historical situation. Christians know that. They also believe that God works in and through history to accomplish his purposes.

Communist philosophy is not flawless. Its ideology is less precise in practice than in theory. Its dogmas are not foolproof. Communist nations are not invincible; their successes are not mathematically predictable. Soviet communism is shaken periodically by inner power struggles in the Kremlin. Red China is a rigid totalitarian state; it is not a cohesive political society. Adaptations, smoldering defiance, and open revolt are inherent in the political life of the satellite states. Communism is not monolithic. Africa has not been captured by the devotees of Marx and Lenin. Presently, Red China and Soviet Russia are locked in a crucial struggle over ideology. The Chinese are "radical"; the Russians are "conservatives." The former are Leninists; the latter are revisionists. That unresolved struggle could throw Russia into the camp of the West. Contemporary history is fluid, not fixed.

Most Americans acknowledge that this is a revolutionary age. Too few, however, seem to understand that black and yellow and brown people everywhere are clamoring for racial, social, economic, and political changes. Lacking a sense of their own history, many Americans "feel" that Africans and Asians are not ready for freedom, that the United States can have one attitude toward western Europe and another toward the rest of the world. They forget that it required a hundred years and a civil war to establish our federal government and that the 1776-81 political-social-economic revolution is still being waged bitterly in some corners of this nation. Charles Malik, speaking at Boston University some years ago, observed that "never have so many people in every corner of the earth reflected so critically upon their present state and projected themselves so hopefully upon the future." [1] The intervening years prove the accuracy of his observation. The historical situation is more fluid in 1966 than in 1950. The map of Africa is dotted with new nations. West Germany and Japan and India and Red China are claiming a place in the sun. Latin America is a stirring giant. Even Canada is edgy at times. And the Negro revolution in America is releasing sociopolitical dynamics which will alter our national image and stance for decades. A new world, for good or ill, is struggling to be born.

Free men everywhere must learn not only to live with revolution but to embrace its creative thrusts and to withstand its debilitating effects. They must especially study and understand the philosophical premises from which the Communist thinks and operates. Free men must face communism's relevant social criticisms and admit that it has a strong appeal to the hordes of hungry, humiliated, frustrated people on three con-

[1] Commencement address, Boston University, June, 1953.

tinents. Free men must keep alert to communism's unswerving determination to force itself on weak governments through false promises, infiltration, and violence. They dare not minimize its totalitarian character which expresses itself in a one-party system, secret police, terrorist gangs, and the liquidation of independent thinkers. They must also identify, assess, and expose communism's weaknesses and failures. Finally, free men, acknowledging their own failures, must demonstrate that personal freedom and social responsibility are compatible in the free world. Here Christianity makes an inestimable contribution. It does not provide a blueprint for action. But it does equip persons to confront the Communist philosophy, program, and passion more effectively than any other "world view." It motivates and enables people to build the good society for the sake of God's kingdom. Christianity *can* overmatch communism.

I. *The Philosophies in Conflict*

Mature Christians admit that grievous social injustices mar human life throughout the world. They recognize, confess, and are seeking to transform a church which has been and is in many places a bulwark of "exclusive" white, middle-class, "Christian" society. But they reject as unrealistic the premise on which communism's social criticism rests—historical materialism. Christians do not despise the material aspects of life. They take the economic interpretation of history seriously, but they do not accept it as the full interpretation. Christianity recognizes the importance of bread; it simply insists that man cannot live by bread alone.

Communism, on the other hand, argues that everyone will be content and happy when he shares in the material things of this world according to his need. Christianity calls that a naïve interpretation of human nature. It views communism's expectations for society as being utopian. The argument that the abolition of capitalistic society will produce, as each earns what he needs, a classless society within the framework of history does not square with reality in Soviet Russia. Christians point to the sharp social cleavages in that Communist state where one class, members of the official party, have supreme power. Communism does not abolish social cleavage; it realigns it. It does not distribute power equitably; it reassigns it to another group. Christianity brands communism's views on man and society unrealistic.

Christianity also rejects as immoral the sly footnote that there need be an "ad interim dictator" while the classless society is emerging. Social, economic, and political power structures must be kept under constant surveillance and evaluated at regular intervals. Because evil resides in persons, *all* social institutions tend toward corruption. Christians argue that the perfect community is not attainable inside history. They orient to the insights in their doctrines of God, man, and eschatology (last things) gaining practical directives there for establishing order, fashioning justice, and making peace.

Christians also oppose Communists because the collectivistic society smothers one's right to property, free speech, and judgments of conscience. Secular man views property in terms of economics, power, and prestige. Christian man, convinced that things exist for persons, argues that the acquisition and use of material goods carries unrealized possibilities for man's growth as a responsible person.

We are not implying that Christianity rises or falls with capitalism. That is not the witness of history.[2] But we are stating

[2] An able exposition of this subject is R. H. Tawney, *Religion and the Rise of Capitalism* (New York: New American Library). See also Nikolai Berdyaev, *Slavery And Freedom* (New York: The Scribner Library), pp. 172-222.

baldly that any society which allows a substantial measure of personal freedom in the economic realm is hospitable to the exercise of Christian stewardship. The concept of private property has theological dimensions. Communism is immoral in its forcible seizure and arbitrary redistribution of private property. Christianity does not endorse an unbridled individualism which flaunts personal ethics and denies social responsibility. But it does support the individual's right to develop through a series of free choices so long as his choices do not infringe on the equal rights of other persons in the community of persons. Communism, denying that right to the individual, is inimical to every political society which allows and safeguards that right by law.

The collectivistic concept inherent in communism reaches far beyond property in its disregard for persons. Communism seeks to control one's mind, shackle his conscience, rule his spirit.[8] Berdyaev observed that Communism's world outlook is "changeless, pitiless, fanatical. . . . It is a philosophy and a religion also." Communism cannot tolerate freedom of mind, conscience, or spirit. It demands that man's thoughts, words, and deeds orient to its rigid doctrines and serve its material goals.

Certainly thought control is not new. It is not confined to Communist countries. The church itself has tried its hand at this despicable practice. The Spanish Inquisition, the excesses in Cromwell's England, and the "witch hunts" in colonial New England are historical proof of that. Nor is this dastardly practice altogether dead. Presently, there are church members who seek to discredit the National and World Councils of Churches, pressure "involved" clergy, and intimidate those who dissent from yesterday's views. But these abortive efforts to control the human spirit are distortions of New Testament Christianity. The majority of churchmen acknowledge that. Communists,

---

[8] Boris Pasternak, *Doctor Zhivago* (New York: Pantheon Books, 1958).

on the other hand, do not view thought control as an evil to be repented of but as a practice to be perfected. In reality, therefore, their philosophy which purports to exalt man actually debases him and dehumanizes society.

Finally, Christianity rejects Communist philosophy because it is atheistic. Everyone knows that Marx called religion "the opiate of the people." Communism views God as an illusion and historical materialism as reality. Lenin, convinced that all religion is outmoded, argued that scientific enlightenment and social order would free men from oppression. Actually, this idealistic sociopolitical philosophy which promises to free man from an authoritarian god subjects him to a rigid, impersonal authority—the ruthless police state.

Communism does not want persons; it makes robots. Christianity does not want robots; it fashions persons. Communism shouts stridently: "Open your door or we will break it down and make you do our bidding." Christ pleads gently: "Behold, I stand at your door and knock. If any man opens the door." The difference between the two "philosophies of life" is chasmic. One humiliates, enslaves man; the other dignifies, liberates him.

II. The Programs Constrasted

What programs do these conflicting philosophies call into being? Plainly defined, the Communist program is amoral. It rests on the view that the end justifies the means. Any means—clever, opportunistic, devious, dishonest—is acceptable if it fosters Communist doctrines and goals somewhere, now or a decade hence. Contemporary political history demonstrates that Communists exhibit few moral scruples, that they intrigue without shame, adapt truth to their own purposes, and employ any means to accomplish the ends they seek. Communists believe that any success gained is a method justified. That is communism's program. Corruption of heart and mind results inevitably.

Contemporary history is filled with the evidences of communism's amoral methods. When the Soviets claimed East Germany after World War II, they used the same methods that the Nazis had employed. They took over former Nazi concentration camps without making any changes. Estimates vary widely, but historians agree that seven to twelve million persons died under forced labor at the hands of the Soviets during and after World War II. The picture in Red China is blurred, but the horror there appears to be incalculable. Communism's program rests on the premise that the end justifies the means. It seeks to disrupt existing governments through false propaganda, subversive acts, infiltration—indeed, by any means which advance its ends.

Admittedly, the free world "fights fire with fire." It acts too often on the premise that the end justifies the means. But Christianity proceeds on the premise that unless the means are acceptable to God, the end, however worthwhile, will not be acceptable to him. Christianity insists that the right goal must be achieved not only in the right way but for the right reason. Wholesome motivation must shape the method employed. Neither manipulation nor coercion of persons is an acceptable means, however good the end may be.

The Christian program is disarmingly simple. It calls for the Word to confront persons through persons; each in his freedom decides to accept and witness or to reject and ignore or attack. This workable program was the means whereby Christianity overmatched paganism in the Roman Empire and spread into every corner of the world by the dawn of the twentieth century. Committed persons, sharing God's Word with others, remain God's program for winning the world.

Because we are committing ourselves to this biblical program in this congregation, and because hundreds of lay persons are working at it, one need not press the argument here. Bit by bit, we are learning experientially that the Christian program calls for persuasive words and sacrificial deeds. To welcome persons from minority groups into one's neighborhood, to challenge those who equate God's gift of new life with the affluent life, to say a good word for Christ in one's home and to speak for him "where cross the crowded ways of life"—these are pieces in Christianity's workable program. Adopting and adapting the program to various situations, every Christian accepts his responsibility to participate in it. Committed persons sharing God's Word *is* the Christian program.

III. Concerning Commitment

Finally, communism, like any human venture, rises or falls on the commitment of its constituency as well as its leadership. Hard core Communists are passionately committed. Since 1917 millions of men and women have demonstrated their dedication to the ideas, ideals, and leaders of the "Revolution." The hardships which the Communists endured in revolutionary Russia are a bloody page in modern history. They rewrote that page in communizing China. The rise of communism in the twentieth century is one proof among many that human beings are capable of suffering and sacrificing for a cause.

Jesus said: "If any man will come after me, let him deny himself, take up his cross, and follow me." The church must sound that clarion call. But first, the church must accept and demonstrate that suffering is the cost of Christian witness. Convinced that neither life nor death nor communism nor nuclear war nor anything else can separate them from the saving love of God, Christians suffer for Christ's sake. They are convinced that Christ uses them to establish beachheads for his kingdom in alien territories. They accept his kingdom as a gift and a *task;* they wait for it and *work* for it confident that the present and the future belong to God.

For we are not contending against flesh and blood, but against the principalities, against the powers, against the world rulers of this present darkness, against the spiritual hosts of wickedness in the heavenly places. Therefore take the whole armor of God, that you may be able to withstand in the evil day, and having done all, to stand. (Eph. 6:12-13.)

13

Christian Context for Political Decision[1]

The election of 1964, emotionally overcharged, was not a shining hour in the history of American presidential elections. Lancaster County was decidedly tense—more so than it had been in 1960 over Mr. Kennedy's religion.

Except for the sermon on McCarthyism in 1954, the pulpit had not dealt specifically with any political *personality* during my twelve-year ministry. That significant facet of politics had been treated regularly in pastoral conversations, in staff and vestry meetings, at "Coffee and Conversation with the Clergy," and in forums (1960 religious issue) open to the community.

Increasingly during the autumn of 1964 conscience and judgment pointed to the pulpit for an appraisal of the presidential candidates and the issues. My ordained associates at Trinity and the members of the official board whom I consulted (Republicans and Democrats) concurred in that judgment. We did wonder how the sermon would affect the pledging for 1965! Emotions were raw, and Trinity's membership includes not only local political leaders but national political leaders—a Republican National Committee member and a former Democratic member of the State cabinet. We were agreed, however, that Trinity's pulpit could not remain silent.

A decade of biblical preaching stood us in good stead. The sermon was well received throughout the parish and widely discussed. The official board, at its regular monthly meeting, was unanimous in the view that the sermon should have been preached. They considered it objective and restrained. Some stated bluntly that Trinity's pulpit would have "failed the parish and the community" if the issues in the 1964 presidential election had not been faced squarely. One family —briefly in Trinity—withdrew from membership. Several other fami-

[1] See Appendix III, "The Word and the World."

lies were petty. A few reported the sermon dishonestly. That was the sum of it among *Trinity's members*. The congregation proceeded to overmatch the highest pledge budget in its history.[2]

But the response from some corners of the community was harsh. The morning daily paper, *The Intelligencer Journal*, printed the full text of the sermon and the evening paper, *The New Era*, carried a fair report on it. Letters—pro and con—hit both papers, my office, and our home. A few Lancastrians resent the sermon to this day. During the vigorous attacks from one quarter of the community, strong support came forward from Trinity's members, vestry, and staff, and from a number of professors at the local college (Franklin and Marshall) and seminary (United Church of Christ), and from some Presbyterian, United Church of Christ, and Lutheran clergy in the community.

Dostoevsky, in his creative novel *The Brothers Karamazov*, moves the Grand Inquisitor to say to the Prisoner (Christ): "In place of the rigid ancient law, man must hereafter with free heart decide for himself what is good and what is evil, having only Thy image before him as his guide." [3] That puts self-interest, party loyalty, and patriotism into clear perspective: the Christian's final arbiter and guide is Christ.

Accepting the authority of God's Word and recognizing each man's freedom to decide any issue for himself, we propose to bring the national political candidates, parties, issues, and ourselves under the judgment and grace of God. Jesus' clear directive, "Render unto Caesar that which is Caesar's and unto God that which is God's," denies his followers the right to avoid personal involvement in the political arena. Recently, our re-

[2] The reader will recall the introductory statement to sermon 6.
[3] (New York: The Modern Library), p. 264.

spected Amish neighbors appeared in the national capital under constraint of their faith, seeking exemption from the social security laws. It is impossible to separate the Christian faith from basic political concerns and activities or from any other area of life for that matter. "God sent his only begotten Son *into the world*."

In this congregation where the tactics of the late Senator McCarthy were evaluated critically a decade ago, where political forums brought Pennsylvania's senatorial candidates to the community, where the sermon on Rolf Hochhuth's *The Deputy* ("But Silence *Is* Decision") was preached twice in six months to capacity congregations, one need not argue this implication of gospel faith.[4] But there is continuing need to encourage this congregation to bring the gospel to bear on the secular-moralistic mind of this community. Some do witness boldly. Too many, however, keep silent over the bridge table, at work, and in their private clubs. Every person who accepts Christ is under divine constraint to bring his maturing Christian insights and judgments to bear on social issues for the sake of the kingdom of God. Now we are concerned with the 1964 presidential election.

I

First, the love of Christ constrains us to view the candidates compassionately and critically. Those who seek and hold public office—like anyone else who exposes his ideas and programs to public view—open themselves to external and internal pressures. Public officials, school teachers, clergymen, and community leaders who seek to blaze new trails must live with constant pressures. A sensitive, enlightened citizenry will strive to make those pressures constructive.

---

[4] See Fisher, *From Tradition to Mission*, chap. 3, "Confrontation and Response."

This pulpit has called periodically for responsible persons to enter public life. It has supported those who hold (or have held) places of leadership in both parties, in local and state governments, and in community affairs. It has encouraged the citizenry to view its public officials and community leaders compassionately. In the tragic hour of President Kennedy's assassination the pulpit commented on the built-in risks of the presidential office and urged the citizenry to view their elected officials with greater maturity and respect for the responsibilities inherent in these offices.[5]

The incontrovertible evidence that the assassination was managed by an emotionally distressed human being does not blunt the relevance of that plea. Nonetheless, many Americans, sobered only briefly by the assassination, were screaming at one another within a month. The current presidential campaign has hit a new low for ill-founded charges and countercharges. The columnist Roscoe Drummond called it the most irresponsible campaign in recent history. Extremists in both parties have spoken falsehoods and done harsh things. Responsible people in both parties, ignoring the Word of the Lord—"Thou shalt not bear false witness"—have made claims for their candidates and issued charges against the opposing candidates with little regard for the candidates' actual statements and voting records. The gospel constrains us to view our candidates and elected officials compassionately.

The love of Christ also constrains us to view our elected officials critically. Jesus said, "The truth shall make you free." Imperfect people in an imperfect world must labor diligently to discern and do the truth. Discerning and doing the truth calls for clearheaded appraisals of the candidates' concrete proposals, their plans for implementing those proposals, and their

[5] For the specific comments see sermon 16, pp. 200-201.

actual voting records. Open inquiry, discussion, debate, and responsible compromise are strands in the fabric of effective political action in any free society.

A cursory appraisal of both candidates' campaigns reveals that they have done their share of mud-slinging. Their ardent supporters have had an even larger hand in this dangerous "political sport." The President of the United States and his supporters err when they charge that the Republican candidate is a warmonger. The infamous TV commercial which presented a little girl in an open field, an ominous voice on countdown, and the suggestion of total annihilation is a "scare tactic" which offends all fairminded citizens. Equally untrue and notably destructive is the Republican charge that the Democratic candidate is "soft on communism."

A critical appraisal of the campaign makes it plain that both candidates have made mistakes in political judgment. President Johnson erred when he swept the Bobby Baker affair under the rug. That decision tarnished his image with many citizens. Mr. Goldwater—nominated by a disciplined minority at San Francisco who exhibited closed-mindedness toward several responsible Republican leaders—made a serious error in his acceptance speech, frightening millions in his own Party.

The disposition of both candidates to exploit the opposition's political mistakes has blurred—at times obscured—the crucial issues which confront the electorate. Millions of Americans look back nostalgically to the presidential election of 1960 when two ambitious young men, conducting their campaigns with dignity, made an honest effort to discuss the issues. But they do not subscribe to the view of the Very Rev. Francis B. Sayer, Dean of the Episcopal Cathedral in Washington, who called for a "plague on both your houses." The Dean dismissed Mr. Johnson as a political cynic and Mr. Goldwater as a man of massive ignorance. Such sweeping judgments do not help the voter make a decision. Nor are they fair. Actually, both candidates appear to be intelligent, decent, patriotic, hard-working. Both are experienced in the ways of the federal government.

Critical-minded Christians will decline to appraise the character (inner motives) of any candidate. "Let him who is without sin cast the first stone" is a relevant admonition in these frenzied days. But responsible Christians will evaluate the *temper of mind* exhibited by each candidate. One facet of Mr. Johnson's mind was revealed when he selected a controversial figure as his running mate—an intellectual, a man with a sharp public image, a dynamic personality. A facet of Mr. Goldwater's mind came into clear view when he selected as his running mate a man whose leadership qualities had not caught the public eye during that man's fourteen years in the Congress. The vice-presidential choices must be judged as potential presidents. Mr. Kennedy's assassination in particular and the uncertainty of life in general constrain the electorate to examine carefully the proven abilities and potentialities of both vice-presidential candidates.

The presidential candidates' tempers of mind can be appraised best by examining their support or rejection of fundamental campaign issues. This is the firm ground on which responsible voters will make their choice, as they should in any election.

II

The love of Christ constrains churchmen to recognize and examine several political issues in this campaign which are inherently moral issues. Critical judgment should direct every citizen to make an appraisal on this ground.

1. God created man free and equal before him. When man rejected that heritage, God's Son died on Calvary to empower the human will to reclaim it. Any political constitution and

any piece of legislation which helps any man reclaim his heritage as a person is endorsed as a matter of Christian conscience. Responsible government seeks to enact laws which provide justice for all its citizens. Admittedly, neither legislation nor responsible law enforcement can create good will in the hearts of men, but these human activities can provide conditions which are hospitable to justice. The problem posed by minorities (Indians, Orientals, Negroes) is a complex one for any political society. It is especially complex in the free society. There are no easy solutions. But the proposed civil rights legislation is one piece in that solution. Every churchman whose conscience is captive to the Word of God acknowledges *that* and will act accordingly. The State is ordained by God to provide machinery to establish justice for all citizens. One candidate has pledged himself to use federal power for that purpose; the other opposes that use of power. You must decide whom to support.

2. At the heart of God's creative and redemptive purposes is his abiding concern for the dignity of the individual. Christ came to restore the whole person. The New Testament ethic calls Christians to bear their own burdens insofar as they are able. It also calls them to bear one another's burdens insofar as human need and human dignity require it. The care of aging persons, economic aid for promising students, and economic help to improve the opportunities for situationally hard-pressed people constitute a moral issue. Practical response to this moral imperative through government aid and community services calls for study, imagination, discussion, debate, and responsible direction. Men will differ on the methods, but the fact that human needs must be met is not, on moral grounds, open to debate.

At this critical juncture in history—when unprecedented social, economic, political, and technological problems confront this nation and other nations—one candidate argues vigorously and has voted consistently for the reduction of federal power in deference to states' rights. His views must be judged by historical realities: wherever the states' rights doctrine is *exalted* there is exploitation of persons (multiple evidences in Alabama and Mississippi). Mr. Goldwater's attacks on federal authority collide with the march of our national life. His views are also at odds with the formative principles of the Republican Party and its creative accomplishments under the leadership of Mr. Lincoln. Mr. Johnson is firmly committed to the principle of federal authority.

Responsible citizens in both parties appreciate that the principle of federal authority must be handled with imagination and restraint. But any suggestion that one can turn back history's clock is not "conservatism"; it is neurotic response to reality. Politically viewed, it is a radical attack on the Republican principles of 1860 and the principles of the Federalist Party which structure our federal government. The repeal of present federal legislation would create economic havoc in some states, endanger thousands of lives in others, and provide privileged sanctuaries for vested interests in still others. Consequently, a constitutional issue in this campaign becomes in fact a moral issue. Both candidates have made their positions clear. You must decide whom to support.

3. Human life, originating at the creative hand of God and defying duplication, calls for preservation at all costs except personal surrender of God's truth. Jesus said, "Fear not those who can kill the body but those who can kill the spirit." Within that broad context peace in this nuclear age is a moral issue. Obviously, there are many serious threats to peace in this revolutionary age. Communism is one of them, but it is not the only one. Nor has it become a sudden threat during this campaign simply because one candidate talks about it. Communism became a potential threat in 1850. It has been a real threat

since the Russian revolution in 1917. It continues to be a serious threat wherever it concretes itself in sovereign states. Presently, it is a serious threat in China.

This pulpit has viewed communism seriously throughout the twelve years of this ministry. Occasional charges by emotionalists in the community that we are not alert to this threat are untrue. In 1954 there was a Freedoms Foundation Award for a straightforward, factual sermon titled, "Christianity and Communism Confront Each Other." Across the years we have called for a flexible but realistic Christian stance toward communism. On biblical grounds we rejected Bertrand Russell's "better Red than dead." We have argued consistently for open negotiations and open agreements between the free nations and the Communist states. We are on record as favoring the recognition of Red China. We questioned the first nuclear test ban as unrealistic (proven so) and supported the present ban as a realistic first half step.

We have argued steadily that it is our political responsibility to coexist with honor while our way of life wins new converts and while Communist nations lose their hold on persons or alter their ideology. That victory could take a century. We have said again and again that the "cold war" is a tough strand in this revolutionary world, that there is no sudden thaw in sight, that no party has a magical solution. Unreservedly, we have supported the United Nations. We have endorsed the several alliances between and among free nations as temporary national policy in a fluid world of sovereign states. Pointing steadily to the irreconcilable differences between Christianity and communism, we have called for a government and citizenry flexible enough to hold inevitable political collisions in "peaceful tension." We have supported national leaders in both parties who displayed restraint, judgment, and cool-headedness in directing this nation which has power primacy in an unstable world community. We supported President Kennedy when he probed into the Cuban situation, spoke cautiously while he examined the frightening alternatives which faced this nation, and then boldly confronted Soviet Russia. We have argued that power can be used constructively by free nations.[6]

There is no reliable evidence that either presidential candidate is "soft on communism" or is a "warmonger." But when the voting records of Senator Johnson and Senator Goldwater are examined, and when their public statements before and during this campaign are examined, the choice before the electorate seems unmistakably plain. It is disturbing that neither candidate has discussed foreign policy in the serious style of the late John F. Kennedy. But one candidate does give evidence of calling forward a responsible advisory group on these crucial matters; the other does not. Honorable coexistence in this nuclear age is a moral issue. The stance and style of each candidate is plain. You must decide whom you will support.

Now a word about that publicized pseudoissue—"morality in government." Centuries ago Martin Luther declared flatly that it would be better to have a wise Turk at the head of the government than a foolish Christian. Competence, judgment, restraint, and cool-headed decisiveness are indispensable for effective national leadership. Political skill, as Mr. Lincoln demonstrated, is a particularly valuable asset in any national leader.

Further, this government is not the arbiter of morals. It exists to provide order and justice, to maintain the political framework within which citizens can mature as responsible persons. It is not the business of any government to prescribe a "national morality." Morality results from one's relationship with God,

---

[6] See Fisher, *From Tradition to Mission*, pp. 60-69, 93-100, 111, 138-45.

or, if one has no existential relationship with God, from one's inner system of values. Like millions of Americans, I recoil from the Bobby Baker and Billy Sol Estes scandals. I was also offended by the scandal set off by former President Eisenhower's assistant, Sherman Adams. But these are peripheral issues. They are "messy situations" to be cleaned up and guarded against in *every* administration.

The "Puritan ethic" will not be restored to American society by either candidate; the ethic no longer dominates our religionized-secular culture. Pluralism is the dominant factor. The plea, "morality in government," is naïve; it can be dangerous, diabolical. If the moral climate in this nation is to change, it will be altered not because a particular man is President of the United States but because the people in this and other American communities choose to adopt more refined and responsible moral standards for themselves, exercise self-discipline, and teach ethical responsibility to their children.

III

Finally, the love of Christ constrains us to examine and assess the bruises and wounds inflicted on the body politic during this presidential campaign. Because of extremists in both parties and irresponsible campaigning by persons in both parties and because of the frustrations, fears, and hostilities in every corner of contemporary America, this campaign has set neighbor against neighbor, friend against friend, and, too often, churchman against churchman. It has widened the chasm between the devotees of two political philosophies—federal power and states' rights—constitutionally intended to exist in tension rather than in chasmic conflict. Abraham Lincoln speaks relevantly to our generation: "With charity for all; with firmness in the right, as God gives us to see the right, let us strive on . . .

to bind up the nation's wounds." It is imperative that many take his words to heart, act on them, and teach their meaning to the new generation. Presently, there is a deep sickness in the body politic. Its cause, not its symptoms, must be treated if this nation is to exercise responsible leadership in the world.

We should also seek to understand, act on, and teach our children what Woodrow Wilson meant when he said, "It is a difficult thing to live the life of a free people." If it was difficult in his day, it is staggering in our day. Let us recognize that simple solutions matched against complex social, economic, political, and technological problems will breed frustration in our citizenry, undermining their confidence in the processes of democratic government. That may prove to be the most crucial issue in this political campaign.

If the United States—too little concerned about what it means to preserve and enlarge this land as the home of the brave and the free—depends on a citizenry which fashions government simply in terms of easing conflicting self-interests rather than in getting at the root of socioeconomic problems, then this nation, like imperial Rome, will fall because it went to pieces at the seams. Presently, the United States is the *only nation with power primacy* in which a majority of the citizens are free to examine political issues critically and to determine for themselves how basic human rights can be guaranteed by law and responsible force to the greatest number of people here *and* abroad.

Each must decide these issues for himself. How will you decide?

IV

beyond
the pulpit

Life is not lost by dying;
Life is lost Minute by Minute, day by dragging day
In all the thousand small, uncaring ways.

—Stephen Vincent Benet

Where cross the crowded ways of life, . . .
We hear thy voice, O Son of man.

—Frank Mason North

14

Why Bother to Do Good?

In spite of current criticisms of the church, parish pastors are still respected in most quarters of American society. Many are invited to address pluralistic groups in America's religionized culture—service clubs, PTA's, patriotic organizations. Some are also invited to address labor-management groups, military gatherings, advertising executives, economists, political clubs, academic gatherings, etc.

The pulpit and the public platform, however, are not interchangeable. An evangelical sermon and a serious public address are different vehicles for truth. Addressing hundreds of pluralistic gatherings in and beyond Lancaster across two decades, I have sought to respect the sensibilities of persons whose religious convictions differ from mine. But the prophetic view of history and the evangelical stance are integral parts of the Christian faith. Every Christian must speak for God wherever he goes. His style and thrust will vary from situation to situation, as it does from parish to parish, but his witness will be made.

This particular address has been employed in various pluralistic gatherings, especially at high school commencements. In addition to the three addresses included in this section *and* the sermons, "God and the 'Organization Man'" and "Can Christianity Overmatch Communism?" (Part III), these subjects have been dealt with in pluralistic gatherings: "The 'New Morality,'" "Bible Reading in the Public Schools," "The Essentials of Mental Health," "Revelation and Reason," "The Right of Dissent in a Free Society," "The Church since 1914," "The Pastoral Counselor and the Helping Professions," "Fundamentalism, Liberalism, and the Bible," "Conscience and Nuclear Testing," "Albert Camus: Preacher to the Disenchanted," "How to Be a Bad Parent," etc.

A steady stream of correspondence across the years reflects the dialogue stirred by this ministry beyond the pulpit. The response has heightened one preacher's cultural awareness, sharpened his evangelical witness, and increased his sense of urgency to proclaim the Word relevantly.

Some questions which we ought to ask—"What can I do to enlarge the province of racial justice?"—we often avoid. Other questions which dissipate our energies—"Why bother to do good?"—we often succumb to.

"Why bother to do good?" Everyone struggles with that nagging question from time to time. With the world as it is, why bother to work hard? Why bother to be kind? Why bother to be decent? Why bother to do good? Indeed, why bother! In one form or another this question dogs our daily round. Many ask it listlessly. Others ask it with thinly veiled defiance. Some fling it out in cold anger. Every generation wrestles with the question: Since affairs are as they are, why should one bother to do good?

How does one argue effectively against this cancerous attitude? Indeed, how does one keep from succumbing to it himself? How does one fight off the weariness that comes with well-doing?

I

Be honest. We shall be helped immensely if we are honest with history. We are not the first generation to have rough going. Fair-minded people are steadied and challenged when they recall how other generations handled themselves in the face of personal and social hardships.

When Thomas Jefferson was elected President of the United States, the New England Federalists hid their Bibles, closed the shutters on their windows, and remained close to their shops and little factories. They believed their own political propaganda which had argued that the country would go to pieces if it fell into the hands of "those Jacobin atheists."

The first decade in nineteenth-century America was uneasy, turbulent, violent. Tensions mounted and conflict stirred as the young nation, having achieved its political independence, set out to win economic independence from England and expand the social-political revolution at home. The continuing struggle over the issue of federal government versus states' rights was so severe that it cost the Federalists their identity; it cost John Randolph of Virginia his sanity; it cost Alexander Hamilton his life. Aaron Burr, discredited after his infamous duel, concocted a scheme to set up a rival government in the west. His plan failed. He was tried for treason and acquitted amidst angry passions. New England, hard hit by Jefferson's Embargo Acts, considered secession from the Union. These internal tensions and conflicts were sharpened by the British who, engaged in a life and death struggle with Napoleon, impressed American seamen and stirred the Indians along America's western frontier. Finally, the turbulence boiled up into the War of 1812. But for the responsible words and deeds of Hamilton and Jefferson and Madison and the two Adamses, father and son, and thousands more, the young republic would have foundered.

A quarter of a century earlier, America's "revolutionary cause" almost faltered because so many Colonials declined to fight. Enlisting and keeping an army prompted the pamphleteer, Tom Paine, to stigmatize the deserters and short-termers as "summer patriots." The American Revolution, idealized for a century, was in reality a bitterly waged "civil war." One third of the Colonials actively supported the war for political independence. Another third were loyal to Britain. The others refused to bother with it at all! Certainly those who stuck it out were haunted by the question, "Why bother?" But they did not throw in the sponge. Our debt to them is incalculable.

When the Black Plague swept across western Europe in the second half of the fourteenth century, entire villas and towns were wiped out. The records are not accurate and scholars' estimates vary, but it appears that half the population of western Europe died within a decade. The specter of anarchy forced community after community to conscript workers. One needs little imagination to reconstruct the picture of young people and oldsters throwing morality to the winds and taking a last fling before the Plague felled them. Those youth who stuck with the books at the "new" universities of Paris and Oxford and Bologna displayed magnificent fortitude. And the adults who kept at their farming, carpentering, weaving, and smithing in those dark years proved their mettle. Because this hard core did stick with the books and farming and carpentering and weaving and smithing, western Europe was able to recoup its energies and claim its resources. Within a century the Renaissance and the Reformation, discovery and colonization, provided the dynamics which enabled western Europe to colonize North America and to dominate Asia and Africa without challenge until the twentieth century.

The second- and third-century Romans who gave their energies to the pursuit of pleasure rather than to constructive social and political tasks hold the spotlight for throwing in the sponge in time of crisis. They did little to steady the Empire which was coming apart slowly at its seams. Here and there a noble Roman such as Marcus Aurelius placed purpose before pleasure, but it was those Christians scattered throughout the Empire who went about doing good. In one sense they held the Western world together. Western civilization was forged during the succeeding thousand years from Greco-Roman culture and Judeo-Christian faith and traditions.

We are not suggesting that ours "is the best of all possible worlds." It is not; it leaves much to be desired. In fact, there is strong evidence that contemporary culture is more dehumanizing than medieval culture was at its worst. It is also true that contemporary problems (local, national, international) are more critical than those in preceding eras because sovereign states presently possess the technological capabilities to devastate the world. Twenty-eight preceding civilizations have died; the twenty-ninth could be blasted to oblivion. There is an incalculable difference between laying siege to a castle and leveling New York or Moscow or Peking with one swift nuclear thrust. Human freedom is always "dreadful freedom." It is notably "dreadful" in this era of unprecedented technological change and revolutionary movements.

This is not the best of all possible worlds, but it is the only world we have. Our willingness to be honest with history can be helpful. The knowledge of other people in other trying times, doing good, can challenge the hero in many a man.

II

Be realistic. Honesty leads to and calls for realism. Elton Trueblood has observed that any alternative to doing good will be socially destructive and self-defeating. If, fatalistically, we spurn personal morality, refuse the responsibility of a sound marriage, decline the privilege of rearing children, and neglect to give our best vocationally in these troubled times, the cumulative effect of our noninvolvement will be to deepen the current mood of futility. In the course of this debilitating process one defeats himself and smothers constructive social dynamics. Thucydides, an ancient Greek historian, argued that whatever men consider to be inevitable finally comes to pass. In any season, but especially in time of crisis, the only constructive possibility is to do good. The alternative—doing nothing—hastens the outcome one dreads.

When the encircled German armies at Stalingrad realized that Hitler considered them to be expendable, both the leaders and the men lost heart; mass surrender resulted. In 1940 when common sense suggested that Britain's skimpy Royal Air Force, overmatched by a superior Luftwaffe, could go through the motions of resistance and, honor appeased, retire from the skies, the RAF elected instead to fight furiously, gallantly, expendably. They did not entertain the widely held view that Britain's defeat was inevitable. They stopped the Luftwaffe cold. Their victory gave the free nations the precious time they needed to build and launch their "crusade" against the Third Reich. The men at Corregidor, Guadalcanal, and the Coral Sea—all expendable—kept the door open to an eventual American victory in the Pacific. Marshall Petain—tired, confused, disillusioned—handed France to the Nazis after six weeks of war. DeGaulle and millions of Frenchmen refused to accept that deed. Branding "Nazi invincibility" a myth, they marched into liberated Paris four years later. The darkness of the Third Reich had covered the city of light for only four of those boasted thousand years!

Losing heart in the face of hardship seals the dreaded outcome. Fatalism breeds defeat and destruction. Doing good in spite of setbacks is not "pollyannish"; it is the only sane, realistic alternative to accepting defeat. Realism counts the cost; but it never counsels surrender simply because the going is rough. On May 28, 1940, during the fall of France, Churchill said bluntly, "The House [Commons] should prepare itself for hard and heavy tidings." [1] And in his public address before the House of Commons a few days later (June 4) he declared boldly: "We shall go on to the end, we shall fight in France . . . , we shall

---

[1] Churchill, *Their Finest Hour* (Boston: Houghton Mifflin Company, 1949), p. 99.

defend our island, whatever the cost may be, we shall fight on the beaches, we shall fight on the landing-grounds, we shall fight in the fields and in the streets, we shall fight in the hills; we shall never surrender." [2]

Disciplined minorities write the pages of human history—for good *and* ill. The American Revolution and the Nazi scourge were *minority* movements. The outcome of World War II was not determined by the fall of France, the debacle at Dunkerque, the surrender of Corregidor. Raleigh's "Lost Colony," and later, the hard winters at Jamestown and Plymouth did not dissuade the English from establishing their influential Atlantic community. Authentic Christians—after nineteen costly centuries—are still working to create the good society for the sake of the kingdom of God. Realism calls one to do good. Otherwise, the triumph of evil is assured.

III

Be humble. Doing good requires honesty and realism. It also calls for humility. Life is not a hundred-yard dash; it is a relay race. No one person or single generation can achieve social justice or fashion world peace. Every man and generation is indebted to the stalwarts of yesteryear. Each person and generation is under obligation to pass the baton to the next generation at an advanced point—if that is possible. The only contribution that some generations can make, however, is to stay in the race; substantial gains are beyond them.

Across three centuries the Romans exchanged personal integrity, political skill, and culture for bread, circuses, and debauchery. That exchange affected the course of civilization adversely for a thousand years. On the other hand, when Britain stood alone for a season against the Nazi juggernaut,

[2] *Ibid.,* p. 118.

her "finest hour" challenged and chastised free men everywhere. It also blunted the Nazi thrust. If our present generation and our children's generation can accomplish coexistence with the Communist bloc, honorably avoiding nuclear war, civilization and humanity can be kept "in the running." That accomplishment, in the perspective of history, may be our most significant contribution.

Humility—which motivates one to see life in terms of others and to assume responsibility for them and for unborn generations—is characteristic of those who do good. The humble man accepts responsibility *now* because he takes the long view of history. Unlike Louis XV of France ("After me, the deluge"), he asks whether a particular national policy will help the next generation live and work in freedom. Unlike today's "status seekers" he asks whether the personal image he projects is salutary for his children and his contemporaries.

Viewed at a deeper level, humility enables one to distinguish between self-reliance and reliance on God and to seek the latter. It encourages one to recognize that God is in as well as beyond history, that God's ways do prevail. Humility moved Mr. Lincoln to call both North and South to acknowledge their joint responsibility to rebuild the shattered nation, not after the dictates of the victorious Republican Party or the impoverished Southern aristocrats, but "as God gives us to see the right." His counsel was ignored. We are reaping the whirlwind today.

> Though the mills of God grind slowly,
> yet they grind exceeding small.[3]

Right is *not* forever on the scaffold; wrong is *not* forever on the throne. The thousand-year Third Reich lasted a decade. The barbarians did not engulf Europe after the fall of Rome.

[3] F. von Logau, "Retribution."

The victory of communism is not inevitable. No marriage is destined to fail. Poverty can be eliminated. Racial injustice can be obliterated. Broadly viewed, world order can be established. "The mills of God grind slowly."

Humble men believe that God overrides man's pompous, dishonest, cruel deeds and that he fosters and enlarges man's fumbling efforts to do good. Isaiah, caught in violent political upheaval, testified:

> The grass withers, the flower fades;
> but the word of our God will stand forever (40:8).

Truth, crushed to earth, is raised by God himself. Those who embrace this view and hold fast to it are enabled to live creatively. Paul, convinced that God overmatches evil, faced personal hardship, social decadence, and political instability with infectious confidence: "So, we never lose heart." Bonhoeffer, imprisoned for his part in the bomb plot on Hitler's life, ministered joyously to his fellow prisoners until early May, 1945, when he was hanged. Doctor Tom Dooley "never, never, never" gave up until cancer snuffed out his life. Martin Luther King, enduring hardship, is indefatigable in his quest for social justice. Humility—the conviction that God is at work in history and that his victory is sure—encourages and prods men to do good.

Neither the bleakest day nor the darkest night disheartens or intimidates those
> who dare to be honest,
> who strive to be realistic,
> who find the courage to be humble.

They go right on doing good, come what may.

15

$\mathcal{L}$t. Ben Toland Wrote a Will

This preacher wrote this address for himself. I have employed it in many places on the assumption that others also need heroic examples. The hero here is Marine Lieutenant Benjamin Rush Toland who was killed instantly on a barren, windswept ridge on Iwo Jima, February 21, 1945.

Shortly after World War II the National Association of Manufacturers produced a flyer on Ben Toland which came to my attention in 1951.[1] His person and example (described in the address) irritated, confused, haunted me. How could any youth achieve his maturity in twenty-three brief years? I tried to forget Ben Toland. I could not. One day I took him as an example of authentic personhood. He influenced my decision in 1952 to forego the completion of a doctoral dissertation in history, to resign the personally hospitable pastorate at College Church, Gettysburg, and to accept the pulpit of Lancaster's downtown, historic "Old Trinity," a parish which experienced colleagues insisted was dying. I looked on Trinity—1952 to 1956—as my "barren, windswept ridge." In those years, remaining at Trinity was a disciplined act of faith.

This address—delivered for community Memorial Day services, at high school commencements, for service clubs, and in military gatherings—has heartened some, challenged others, angered a few. The dialogue it evokes is stimulating, revealing, enriching.

In the late 1950's Trinity decided to provide a Memorial Day Sunday service (May 30). The Bach chorale gave way to Fred Waring's arrangement of "The Battle Hymn of the Republic"; the minister of music produced a brass ensemble; the hymns were militant ("Onward, Christian Soldiers," "A Mighty Fortress"). The sermon, taking the

[1] "Faith," (New York: National Association of Manufacturers, n.d.). See also "Lt. Rush Toland Memorial Study No. 1," in Paul Pigors, *Effective Communication in Industry* (New York: National Association of Manufacturers, 1949). All quotes from these pamphlets are used by permission.

story of Ben Toland as an extended introduction, presented the gallant Jesus on his "collision course" with Calvary, reviewed the cost of our salvation, and probed at our persons, asking whether they demonstrated the power of Christ's resurrection. The exciting response to that service set the style for similar services across the years.

On Iwo Jima, on February 21, 1945, Lt. Benjamin Rush Toland assumed command of a fellow officer's platoon, took the assigned ridge, and was killed instantly while laying out air markers. He invites remembrance and emulation not simply because he died heroically but especially because he lived purposefully.

Ben Toland was able-bodied, handsome, socially gracious, intellectually gifted, emotionally mature. He achieved a brilliant social, athletic, and scholastic record in the several schools he attended. In preparatory school, St. Paul's, he distinguished himself. At Yale University he was co-captain of the freshman hockey team and an active participant in football and tennis. He was a recognized leader in student affairs. Elected to Phi Beta Kappa in his junior year, he received his bachelor's degree *summa cum laude*. Ben Toland, a five-talent man, put his innate gifts and splendid cultural advantages to creative use during his brief life.

Graduating when his nation was embroiled in World War II, he volunteered with the United States Marines. Commissioned a Second Lieutenant in the United States Marine Corps Reserve, he was assigned as an aide to General J. C. Underhill, assistant division commander, Fourth Marine Division, a position of comparative safety. Some men deliberately sought staff assignments; some who received them held to them tenaciously. But Ben Toland clamored for combat duty. Eventually, his request was granted. He was wounded on Saipan. Recovered, he returned eagerly to combat duty. On February 21, 1945, he was killed instantly on Iwo Jima.

Because Benjamin Rush Toland—and others like him—was willing to die, people in the free world can worship God, speak openly, and write critically without fear of personal reprisal. Certainly that is substantial reason to remember Ben Toland and the 390,000 other men and women who died to secure our freedom. But there is more to Ben Toland's story. This young man died in an act beyond the call of simple military duty. This is how a surviving fellow Marine recalled Lt. Toland's death that day on Iwo Jima. "I was with Ben on Iwo. His platoon was already in its position. And no one ordered him to take command of the other platoon. He just knew the officer was wounded—and somebody had to do the job. . . . He charged the ridge—and took it. Was laying out air markers when the Jap mortar shell hit. . . . That's the story." [2]

"That's the story." Indeed! The story is pregnant with meaning for this generation of careful, calculating men. Ben Toland was the kind of man who makes the difference between victory and defeat on the battlefield, who spells the difference between social progress and social stagnation in days of peace. Ben Toland's voluntary deed on Iwo reflects a bit of Jesus' free spirit: "No man takes my life from me. I lay it down of my own accord."

Few people are endowed as lavishly as was Ben Toland. Yet he, possessing multiple gifts and having had unusual opportunities to develop them, did not consider himself too valuable to die for freedom and for humanity. He exercised a responsible stewardship over God's exciting gifts to him. Whoever chooses to live an unimaginative, adaptive, indulgent life—and many do—must blot out the memory of Ben Toland and people like

[2] Ibid., p. 3.

him. But if a majority among us manage this terrible forget-fulness—which can be accomplished through mundane thoughts and words and deeds day after day—then men such as Ben Toland will have died in vain. Ben Toland haunts me. Let him haunt you, too.

But there is more to Ben Toland's story. Listen to the rest of it, the best of it. Before Ben Toland died on that barren, bloody slope on Iwo Jima, he had no opportunity to speak a final word to others. In a split second, life was ripped from his strong body by that exploding mortar shell. He died in the twinkling of an eye without a word to anyone.

Others have had the precious privilege of saying a last word before death, a privilege that some covet and a few use mag-nificently. Nathan Hale, Revolutionary patriot, has captivated generations of sensitive Americans with his bold words before he was hanged as a spy by the British: "I regret that I have but one life to give for my country." But Ben Toland was denied that privilege of speech before death closed in relentlessly. Yet being dead, he speaks eloquently. Ben Toland wrote a will! It was discovered among his effects, a penciled document, writ-ten on December 20, 1943, just fourteen months before his death.

"I, Benjamin Rush Toland, a legal resident of Concord, New Hampshire, USA, now in the active naval service as a First Lieutenant, U. S. Marine Corps Reserve, and being of sound and disposing mind and memory and not acting under duress, menace, fraud or undue influence of any person whatsoever do set this down as the instrument of my last will and testament." [3] The preamble reads like any well-framed will. Thereafter, it is unique. More than any last words, that simple document is an expression of his faith in God and man, and a continuing chal-

[3] *Ibid.,* p. 1.

lenge to sensitive people everywhere. This is the substance of Lt. Toland's last will and testament:

—To his beloved Episcopal Church Ben Toland left a share in his estate, "to bring the Kingdom of God nearer to earth—and earth nearer the Kingdom of God."

—With firm faith in the potential of critically trained minds, he left equal parts of his estate to St. Paul's School and to Yale University, "to promote research toward solution of contemporary problems." For he knew that another generation would need that kind of training if sound solutions to this world's problems were to be found.

—He left a share of his estate to the Congress of the United States, charging that body to govern in the interests of all people, to build a farsighted foreign policy, and to foster international trade and international cooperation so that all nations might have the opportunity to develop their personal and material resources.

—Finally, with faith in the possibility of man's disciplined understanding of himself and of others, he left one share of his insurance to the CIO and to the AFL and another share to the National Association of Manufacturers to "promote understanding of problems of employers and cooperative action in their solution." [4]

What a remarkable document that is! Ben Toland's placement of every dollar demonstrates his firm faith in God, in man's critical faculties, in man's disciplined understanding of persons, in a rational and morally responsible democracy. What he wrote was an expression of the man he was. Anyone looking over his shoulder as he penciled that will on December 20, 1943, could

[4] *Ibid.*, pp. 2-3.

have predicted that Ben Toland would go beyond the call of simple duty, that he would travel the second mile, no matter what it cost him. And he did precisely that.

Certainly Ben Toland was not the only man to go beyond the call of military duty during World War II. The young Britons who flew their Spitfires against the overwhelmingly superior Luftwaffe have been immortalized by Winston Churchill. Who can forget General Jonathan Wainwright and the gallant men and women of Corregidor, holding out after all hope of reinforcements had passed? Many men did go the second mile, but only a handful carried an intelligent dream of peace. Fewer still gave disciplined thought to a concrete program for making the brave, new world.

The tragedy in World War II—as in every war—is that so many men deteriorated as human beings while they waged total war. They lost their sensitivity, surrendered inner refinement, mocked the ideal of a responsible humanity. Like the German soldiers of Erich Maria Remarque's unforgettable story of World War I, *All Quiet on the Western Front*, the men of Norman Mailer's *The Naked and the Dead* and Irwin Shaw's *The Young Lions* are men without a dream, without a hope, without a prayer.

And hundreds of thousands who lived through that dread conflict have let themselves be pressured into seeking comfort rather than character. Ben Toland casts a long shadow. His authentic person heartens some, shames others, challenges many. How does it strike you?

Is Ben Toland's life an equitable exchange for your life and mine? He died. Do we deserve to live? How many of us are contributing what Ben Toland would have contributed if he had not died on Iwo Jima? How does your will read and in whose interests is it written? How does mine read? What character of life does your will and mine reflect? And our deeds—*now!* Do they honor a fallen brother of Ben Toland's stature? Or are we the living proof that Ben Toland and others like him died in vain?

These are haunting, humbling, holy questions. Each of us is fashioning his answers day by day. Any of us can be overwhelmed by a life like Ben Toland's. One can argue neatly that he cannot live on that grand scale and thereafter seek comfort among his lackluster contemporaries. Or, any of us can thank God for Ben Toland and employ his own one, two, or five talents in the interests of humanity, thereby demonstrating that yesterday's true heroes—Ben Toland and many like him—did not die in vain.

Is Ben Toland's life an equitable exchange for your life and mine? Well, is it?

16

Memorial Address—John F. Kennedy

Many people remember as though it were yesterday that "black Friday" when the nation's vigorous young President, John F. Kennedy, was cut down by an assassin's bullets. Shock, sorrow, confusion, and righteous indignation rolled over Lancaster as it did the nation. Trinity Church, open seven days a week, had a steady stream of people who sought the sanctuary and the chapel for prayer and meditation.

In consultation with the staff and vestry, it was decided that the Sunday morning services should be conducted as scheduled and that a special service be conducted on Monday in concert with our fellow Christians at St. Matthew's Roman Catholic Church in Washington, D.C. The late noonday service that Monday, November 25, 1963, was attended by two thousand persons who overflowed the sanctuary into the chapel and the parish house. Republican and Democratic leaders (members of the congregation) shared in the service. The memorial address, extensively reported in the two local dailies and broadcast several times that day by a local radio station, was well received by the worshipers and the community. Requests for copies of the address carried it through six printings.

A secretary in the Washington office of Ross Bass, then Representative and now Senator from Tennessee, brought it to his attention. Mr. Bass read it into the *Congressional Record* (December 17, 1963). Two professors from Northwestern University, publishing a collection of addresses by Roman and Protestant clergy and Jewish rabbis, requested and included the address.[1]

Several hundred letters have come in on the Kennedy service, an occasional one still requesting a copy of the memorial address. I have never heard a word in Trinity Church other than appreciative for the

---

[1] Charles J. Stewart and Bruce Kendall, ed., *A Man Named John F. Kennedy* (Glen Rock, New Jersey: Paulist Press, 1964), pp. 184-89.

memorial service and address on that Monday when the free world laid to rest John Fitzgerald Kennedy, concerned, creative, courageous thirty-fifth President of the United States.

John Fitzgerald Kennedy, thirty-fifth president of the United States, projected an image of the splendid American. It is fitting and proper in this Christian service that we take cognizance of his person and his leadership.

In a society of fragmented persons the fullness of President Kennedy's person was striking: intellectual curiosity, moral sensitivity, social consciousness, political sagacity. Unlike many activist leaders Mr. Kennedy was an intellectual. On occasion he could be philosophical such as Jefferson and Lincoln and Wilson had been before him. But in an age when some intellectuals are content to toy with ideas, to fondle them as ends in themselves, John Kennedy was remarkably decisive; he coveted results. Rarely precipitous, often cautious, he cleanly made significant decisions. This rare combination of intellectualism and activism—a vigorous commitment to the "strenuous life" —was reminiscent of another dynamic president, Theodore Roosevelt.

Deep, quiet emotion gave added dimension to Mr. Kennedy's thoughts, public addresses, deeds. Unostentatiously he worshiped the Christian God, honoring Christ's church as a vehicle of God's grace. Few presidents have been as disciplined in corporate worship as the late President. Further, this emotionally healthy man was devoted to his wife and children. He enjoyed to the hilt and accepted responsibly his parental relationships with Caroline and John. His generous, delightful, public recognition of his accomplished wife was positively refreshing. Not least among the Kennedy contributions was the image of an exciting marriage. The Kennedys were indeed America's "first family." May the

Holy Spirit support and sustain that grief-stricken home cruelly broken by an assassin's bullet.

Now an observation on Mr. Kennedy's leadership. No one, of course, can appraise it fairly at this juncture. His administration, launched on an evenly divided vote of the electorate and less than three years old in the moment of his tragic death, had only begun to take shape, to reveal its structure. A later generation of historians will evaluate that structure. But one can venture the judgment that the style of the Kennedy administration will affect future administrations, and that evidences of his strong personal leadership are plainly discernible.

When the Bay of Pigs venture turned into a debacle, President Kennedy accepted full responsibility. That *is* leadership. As Birmingham seethed and exploded regularly, as the "Old South" threatened political anarchy, as the Washington Freedom March took shape, President Kennedy called for the most comprehensive civil rights legislation in American history. He did so in the full knowledge that this would disrupt his party in the South and offend the complacent and bigoted in every corner of America. That *is* leadership. On the international front he resisted the hotheads and ignored the political illusionists. He examined the Cuban situation methodically, spoke cautiously for weeks, studied the frightening alternatives, and then, knowledgeably, took the first bold step toward nuclear war if Soviet Russia continued to use Cuba as a missile base. That daring, realistic confrontation revealed a quality of leadership reminiscent of Mr. Lincoln's costly decision to preserve the Union by force. Honest men differ with John Kennedy's decisions; some charge him with moments of indecision. But no person denies that Mr. Kennedy was a decisive leader. The thirty-fifth President of the United States has won a firm place in that select band which historians call "strong" presidents. May his successor be equally strong.

We remember John Fitzgerald Kennedy as one who exercised responsible leadership and paid for it with his life. We remember his gracious wife who enriched the presidential office in a score of ways, but never so significantly as in the hour of her husband's tragic death. We remember Caroline and John, Jr., whose enthusiastic escapades pointed to a happy family in the White House. We remember Mr. and Mrs. Joseph P. Kennedy who reared their children to avoid casual living and to serve their country in war and peace. Finally, we remember the late President's Roman Catholic Church which taught him the ways of God, sustained him during hard days, and now offers the comfort of the resurrection Christ to his bereaved family.

John Fitzgerald Kennedy—complex person, devoted husband, exuberant father, dedicated citizen, bold leader—projected an image of the splendid American. May the impact of his person inspire America's youthful and adult citizenry to project that image, too. Forgetting, therefore, the things which ought to be forgotten (for the political arena is a bruising place) and remembering the things that ought to be remembered ("Ask not what your country will do for you—ask what you can do for your country"), let us campaign actively for human rights and freedom and honorable coexistence. Those were his aims; they cost him his life. They should cost us something.

But this tragic event—the assassination of a president in a civilized, free society—calls serious citizens not only to remember their fallen leader but to face up to inescapable historical realities.

First, this nation has forgotten in its hour of affluence and mounting cynicism that the office of the President of the United States has built-in risks for any incumbent. Four presidents have been assassinated; three have died in office. One president's wife, Rachel Jackson, died, exhausted by the viciousness of the election campaign. Every incumbent has been harassed, vilified, hindered, hurt. The hour should be at hand when our citizenry view their presidential candidates and elected executives more maturely—giving them sympathetic respect, assessing their awesome responsibilities, cooperating with them intelligently and generously, and learning to pray daily for them. Critical judgments must be made; a free society cannot exist without them. But such judgments can and must be made responsibly, respectfully, fairly, honestly, openly.

Second, no responsible American will view the tragic events at Dallas simply as bizarre happenings. Ignorance, prejudice, envy, and willful self-interest have fanned the fires of hatred in too many places to let Americans rest complacently. These widespread emotional fires not only produce multiple character assassinations by innuendo and shameless slander; they also incite warped persons to infamous deeds: a wall of shame in Berlin; an alien society in Cuba; a murdered Negro leader and the broken bodies of little children in a bombed church in Birmingham; the assassination of an American president on the open streets of an American city; the senseless killing of a Dallas policeman; the vengeful murder of the assassin. Guilt is corporate. Soul-searching and repentance and mended ways must mature our national temper of mind.

Lee Oswald's death will not assuage Jacqueline Kennedy's grief nor restore the father of Caroline and John, Jr. But the Kennedy family can find some creative purpose in the President's death if this nation rises with fresh resolve to work creatively for human rights and freedom and honorable coexistence. That national mood can only originate in and emanate from complex American communities such as Lancaster and Dallas, Philadelphia and Birmingham. Mr. Lincoln speaks to us, a generation mired in arrogance, pride, prejudice, affluence, multiple fears, and ad interim ethics: "With malice toward none; with charity for all; with firmness in the right, as God gives us to see the right, let us . . . bind up the nation's wounds."

Finally, this tragic event reminds Christians that while some human beings can and do emerge as decisive leaders, only Christ has the power to save; that human leaders pass away and only God remains as the ground of all existence; that justice and brotherhood are illusions outside God's kingdom. If, therefore, our citizenry chooses this sad, bleak moment to repent of those things which they have done and ought not to have done, and if our citizenry looks more eagerly to God in the conviction that apart from him they build to no avail, then Mr. Kennedy who lived creatively shall not have died in vain.

Now, we, in the company of our fellow Christians in St. Matthew's Catholic Church in Washington, commit John Fitzgerald Kennedy to Almighty God from whose creative hand he came, and to Christ whose resurrection is his and every man's only hope, and to the Holy Spirit who calls all persons, fashioning those who respond for eternal life.

appendix I

Note Taking on Sermons

Across the years an increasing number of parishioners have asked for mimeographed sermons. We could not, because of a limited staff (until recently) and heavy counseling responsibilities, keep up with the demand. Consequently, we suggested a decade ago that the parishioners take notes during the sermon or later set down the major points from memory. Several years ago the simple format shown on page 204 was provided. The sheets, available in the pew racks, are used regularly. Often in "Coffee and Conversation with the Clergy" (Appendix II) the questioner will bring out *his* set of notes. Parishioners also use their notes for teaching and in evangelizing. Taped sermons have been available since 1961. These are shared regularly with the shut-ins. Others claim various tapes from the files in the parish library for personal use and in evangelistic work.

The Evangelical Lutheran
Church of the Holy Trinity

Lancaster, Pennsylvania

Notes on Sermons

Date: Preacher:

Title of Sermon:

Scripture References:

Major Points of Sermon:

1.

2.

3.

4.

5.

(use other side for additional notes)

appendix II

Coffee and Conversation with the Clergy[1]

On the second Sunday evening of every month, from 75 to 125 persons—parishioners and others—gather in Trinity's Parish House for "Coffee and Conversation with the Clergy." The setting is informal; persons have opportunity before and after the session to meet and to talk with one another.

Anyone, member or guest, is free to speak in "Coffee and Conversation." The moderator (a clergyman, usually the senior pastor) interprets, keeps the discussion from going afield, and summarizes; he does not attempt to control the discussion. This is not "discussion for discussion's sake." Persons are encouraged to think before speaking. Although no effort is made to arrive at a single conclusion, the goal is always to bring theological and biblical insights to bear on a given question.

"Coffee and Conversation" began as a forum for discussing the sermons preached in Trinity during the previous month. However, the areas of concern also include any subject relevant to the Christian faith and life. Abortion, suffering, peace demonstrations, family life, death, suicide, morality—these are a few of the topics that have been aired during the past year. Perhaps the most exciting dialogues have centered about corporate guilt (the month after the assassination of President Kennedy) and "the new morality."

---

[1] This description is by the Rev. Jack R. Hoffman, Assistant Pastor, Trinity Church.

The purpose of "Coffee and Conversation" is to provide persons in the parish an opportunity to ask questions and to voice their thinking about matters that most concern them. Ideas and insights are shared; Scripture and doctrine come alive; persons are nurtured and supported in their efforts to live under the judgment and grace of the Word. As one thrust in a total teaching program, "Coffee and Conversation with the Clergy" has proved to be a deeply meaningful time of dialogue and encounter.

appendix III

The Word and the World

The official board which had framed a statement in support of the open forum on "the religious issue" in the 1960 election fashioned and voted unanimously on the following statement in September, 1964. This statement supported Trinity's open forums which brought both senatorial candidates to speak in the parish hall as well as the pulpit which continued to examine facets of the presidential campaign.

The Vestry of the Lutheran Church of the Holy Trinity, Lancaster, Pennsylvania—accepting the authority of scripture's witness to God's Word, the confessional witness of Lutheranism since 1530, and the Lutheran Church in America's pronouncements in conventions—holds that Christ's Church has not only the right but also the responsibility to call all human affairs before the tribunal of biblical evidence. This confrontation by the Word honors the freedom of any man, group, or society to respond to, ignore, or reject the Word. It is the Word of God which constrains the Church, laity and clergy to speak.

We hold that there are at all times moral issues which must be discussed and moral decisions which need to be defined in the light of God's Word. The Church's loyalty to Christ transcends personal interest, family loyalty, political concerns and, if need be, loyalty to the state, yet it is inextricably related to these human concerns. Concisely put: Christianity cannot be compartmentalized; the Christian person cannot be isolated from society. The task is not easy for the Church in a day when so many—inside and outside the church—desire the Church to remain silent on all but the most narrowly defined "spiritual matters." This is a denial of the Gospel's concern for the whole person and the Church's call to witness. Therefore, the Church, entrusted with the Gospel, resists every effort from within or without to domesticate the precious Gospel of God. Christians will differ as to how the Church's witness shall be made; they cannot, without breaking faith with Christ, decline to make that witness. We are grateful to God that the Church in America, not dependent in any wise on the State for support, is uniquely poised to witness for her Lord.

Finally, we hold specifically that the present vigor and vitality of Trinity parish stem directly from its clerical and lay willingness to enter into Christ's prophetic ministry.

Each vestryman, twenty-one in number, the three ordained clergy, and the lay assistant affixed their signatures to this statement. Read to the congregation and printed in the parish paper, it stirred dialogue in some quarters of the community. The autumn of 1964—like 1962-63 (when the clergy and some of the laity participated in public demonstrations) and 1960 ("religious issue") and 1959 (Bible reading in the public schools) and 1957-59 (thrusts on race culminating in an integrated congregation) and 1954 (critique of McCarthyism)—was tense, exciting, maturing for Trinity's members as they witnessed in and dialogued with the world.